TO Rick From Donna and Kenn

Happy 78th Birthday

we both love
you with all our
hearts :)

50 SHADES OF RUST

BARN FINDS YOU WISH YOU'D DISCOVERED

TOM COTTER

First published in 2014 by Motorbooks, an imprint of Quarto Publishing Group USA Inc., 400 First Avenue North, Suite 400, Minneapolis, MN 55401 USA

Motorbooks titles are also available at discounts in bulk quantity for industrial or sales-promotional use. For details write to Special Sales Manager at Quarto Publishing Group USA Inc., 400 First Avenue North, Suite 400, Minneapolis, MN 55401 USA.

To find out more about our books, visit us online at www.motorbooks.com.

ISBN-13: 978-0-7603-4575-7

Library of Congress Cataloging-in-Publication Data
Cotter, Tom, 1954-
50 shades of rust : amazing barn finds you wish you'd discovered / by Tom Cotter.
    pages cm
ISBN 978-0-7603-4575-7
1. Automobiles--Collectors and collecting. 2. Antique and classic cars--Anecdotes.
3. Automobiles--History. I. Title. II. Title: Fifty shades of rust.
TL7.A1C683 2014
629.2220973--dc23
                              2014013232

Publisher: Zack Miller
Editor: Jordan Wiklund
Design Manager: Brad Springer
Cover Designer: Kent Jensen
Layout Designer: Diana Boger
Cover photography: Lura Lauer
On the front cover: A rusty Jaguar E-Type peeks from beneath a crimson silk sheet. *Lura Lauer* and *Carlos Lopez*.
On the back cover: Learn the secrets of the 1954 Chicagoan (left) and the hidden Triumph Roadster (right) inside.
On the back flap: Author Tom Cotter.

Printed in USA

10 9 8 7 6 5 4 3

This book is dedicated to Dean Jeffries,
the smartest man I've ever met.

These barn-find books are fun to read, but hard to write. I try to keep track of all who helped in the production, but sometimes I leave someone out. A big thanks to Mark Henderson, a barn-finder and storyteller who rolled up his sleeves and wrote a couple of excellent stories. Also to Somer Hooker, the Vincent motorcycle connoisseur, who has contributed a number of stories over the years—thank you, Somer. And my local sports car friend Mitch Goldstein, former MBI editor Wes Eisenschenk, Larry Trepel for his cool cartoon, John Barron for his prize-winning Apollo story, and Pieter Ryckaert. Thanks to my friend and Long Island native Adam White, who turned me on to the cool Jaguar story.

And thanks to my friend Woody Woodruff, who helps me with everything!

Thanks to my editors at Motorbooks International—Zack Miller and Jordan Wiklund—who continue to indulge me in my barn-find passion. Also thanks to Motorbooks' Marketing Manager Nichole Schiele.

Regarding the cover photography, thanks to my neighbor Lura Lauer and Carlos Lopez, both talented UNCC photography students who shot the photo for this front cover—guys, it's gorgeous. Also, Kevin Neild and Bob Lauer, who helped push the Jaguar around during the photo session. Also thanks to Kevin Brown, who loaned me his barn to shoot the photo, and to Travis Freezel, my department head at Belmont Abbey College, who introduced me to his neighbor's barn. And to Franziska Long for loaning me the E-Type.

And finally, thanks to my long-suffering wife, who allows her life to be dictated by my automotive passions.

"It's a miracle—a '37 Bugatti!" Larry Trepel

A FRIENDLY NOTE TO BARN-FINDERS

When picking up your new barn-find, bring a real camera!

After six barn-find books, I see an uncomfortable trend developing. Many people take beautiful glamor photos of their cars when they are fully restored, but few barn-finders take high-quality photos when their find is unearthed.

The publisher requires high-resolution images of 300 dpi and above for prints to be used in these books, and often, the as-found photos are much lower quality than that. When retrieving your new project, remember to bring along a real camera—not just a cell phone camera—so you can take high-quality images of your car from the start.

You'll be in much better shape if you'd like to submit it for a future book, and the before-and-after shots will be that much better on your garage wall.

Thanks,
Tom

CONTENTS

Rust Never Sleeps

by Wayne Carini
Host of *Chasing Classic Cars*, on the Velocity network

Rust and the classic cars have a complicated relationship. Rust can be the bane of the car owner's existence—extensive rust can drive a car to the junkyard or to expensive refabrication and restoration. Rust can render a car dangerous to operate. Even a spot of rust can spell doom to a car owner as it can spread quickly and without regard for make, model, and year. For all of the pain that rust can cause, though, it can also tell the car collector a human story about the lives of the people who drove the car, where they lived, what they did, and what their particular brand of life was like.

In the early days of the automobile, rust was a nuisance, an embarrassment, a cancer that had to be removed. Rust removal did not begin as a concern for the aesthetics of the car but as a utilitarian enterprise. The average automobile was the second largest investment for a family besides a house; it had to last a long time. Early car owners repaired their cars so that the drivetrains could survive long enough to get them from point A to point B. Families did not take their cars in to trade them up for the newest model like we do so often today.

The '40s and '50s saw the birth of the collector car hobby as we know it. Full restoration was in vogue. The mindset in those days was to present a car that looked better than it did the day that it rolled off the assembly line. My father, Robert Carini, began his long career in automotive restoration with a Model A Ford that he found behind a barn in a small Connecticut town. He made that car look brand new, and along with two other friends, founded the Model A Restorer's Club of America.

When my father restored a car, he did it to absolute perfection. From a young age, I helped him in the shop. Whichever car he was working on—be it a Packard, Duesenberg, Buick, Lincoln, or Ferrari—it had to be an award winner. Every year we would pack up and head from Connecticut to Hershey, Pennsylvania, the Mecca of the collector car hobby, with our latest work in tow. These were both exciting and stressful times. Everything about the car we brought had to be absolute perfection. We went as far as to take a jack to the car show, jack the car up, and rotate the wheels so the name on the hubcap was perfectly horizontal and the valve stem was pointed straight up. I cannot recall a time when my father didn't take home a trophy.

For my father, restoration was the ultimate joy in the classic car business. He lived for the details, for giving an old wreck a new lease on life. Being witness to such perfection, and getting a chance to learn hands-on, has been incredibly formative to me and to my work. I too love to restore a car to absolute

perfection, but I find myself being drawn to old barns and garages. Maybe I'm lured by the promise and hope of complete originality, the excitement of finding a piece of history, frozen in time. I don't fear rust—in fact, rust is in itself beautiful, a badge won for a car's survival. My television show, *Chasing Classic Cars*, has given me the unique opportunity to share this passion with viewers. I feel as if I am on a constant treasure hunt for rusty gold, and I've never had more fun.

Tom's books perfectly capture the unhindered joy of what we're now calling automotive archaeology. There's something about finding that car, hearing the stories, and getting a glimpse into not only an automotive history, but also the personal history of the previous owner—it's intoxicating. From all the time that we have been collecting and restoring cars, we have finally caught on to what art collectors have known for years. The piece of art, or in our case the automobile, should be treasured for what it is, in the condition that it is in. If the car shows a little sign of rust because the paint has been worn through, that's all the better. If the interior is worn and the seats have a bit of a tear, it should be left alone. Now we say that these cars have a "patina." Cars with patina tell a story, much like works of art. This has caught on so much that there is now a preservation class at Pebble Beach. Rat Rods are being built out of rusty old car parts and enjoyed by a whole new type and generation of car collector. Cars with surface rust on them are being clear coated to preserve the rust. Things certainly have changed in the past few years. Rust is finally in!

There is always a fear in the back of my mind that we're going to run out of cars to find, that soon every barn will be without rusty gold, but every time this fear rears its head, I'll get a call or an email about a barn full of cars, and I'm on the chase again.

The Art Of The Hunt: It's Human Evolution

As a kid, there was nothing more exciting than when friends and I were "on the hunt," usually for some kind of pirate's treasure or secret hideaway. We never found any, but for a bunch of 12-year-old kids, that didn't matter.

These days, decades older, I get just as excited while following up a hot lead for some sort of automotive treasure, even if I never actually find it. My friend Peter Egan, longtime editor-at-large at *Road & Track* magazine, has a favorite saying: "It's all about the journey, not the destination."

I think I know how he feels. A good hunt gives me an adrenaline rush I can't get anywhere else.

I needed to find out exactly what happens inside the brain of a barn-finder when he's on the prowl. So I spoke with a psychologist who understands both sides of the equation. Geoff Hacker is an industrial psychologist who teaches psychology, interpersonal communications, managerial decision making, and other courses at the university level. But this PhD is also a car-hunter's car hunter.

Hacker, 51, searches for and restores fiberglass specials, homemade sports cars from the 1950s and 1960s often referred to as *kit cars*. He has dozens of one-of-a-kind fiberglass sports cars stored in and around Tampa, Florida. As a professor, Hacker takes a more academic approach to car hunting than most of us. "My hunt is mostly research for new information," he says. "If I find and buy a car in the process, that's even better."

Hacker may call the phone number of an interesting car from a 30- or 40-year-old classified ad. Sometimes he discovers the car never sold. And at the very least, he's had a great many fascinating discussions, and often finds himself the student instead of the mentor.

"For car guys, it seems ownership is not as important as the adventure," he says, putting on his psychologist's hat. "In some regard, we are trying to reclaim our youth, trying to acquire toys of our childhood. For those of us of a certain age, life is just not as exciting as when we were kids."

Hacker makes a distinction between "hunting" and "hoarding," in which individuals acquire many vehicles and keep them for long periods of time, often in a state of continuous disintegration.

"Hunters sell or trade vehicles; hoarders seldom do," he said, quickly adding that he occasionally sells his cars. "The art of the hunt is primarily related to an evolution of human beings," he says. "Think about

it; we are using the word *hunt* to discuss searching for cars. It wasn't too long ago—a couple of hundred years—that we actually needed to hunt and kill the food we ate.

"It's an endorphin release," he adds, "whether killing a wild boar or finding an old Packard, it gives us a similar feeling of mental gratification. You can see the gleam in Wayne Carini's eye when he makes a new discovery on *Chasing Classic Cars*."

Hacker maintains, though, that car hunters today definitely have the advantage over cavemen when they were tracking boar. "Let's face it; we have *Hemmings*

Motor News, online sources, auctions, classified ads, and Google Earth, in addition to simply driving down country roads when looking for old cars."

Then again, finding great cars is still not a simple endeavor, according to Hacker.

"It never fails—the harder I work, the luckier I get!"

Geoff Hacker
Founder of the Forgotten Fiberglass website and automotive archeologist extraordinaire
www.ForgottenFiberglass.com

I

FOREIGN
AFFAIRS

CHAPTER 1
The Dark Belgian Sanctuary

by Pieter Ryckaert

In 1938, Belgian Roger Van Caneghem was literally born amongst cars. His father had enough passion and mechanical know-how to be totally engulfed by cars, littering every nook and cranny of his house with cars and parts, and the tools and materials to work on them.

This passion became so dominant, the family house nearly collapsed as the ceiling started to come down from the weight of axles and engines upstairs. So after World War II, in 1948, nobody was surprised when Roger's father set up his own garage repair shop. Roger learned the trade from a very young age, as he spent all his time in his dad's garage.

Along with daily mechanical work, father and son grew very fond of Peugeots. They began collecting them. They snapped up several models, as the postwar years had left lots of abandoned cars for the taking. But even at that time, the price of Peugeots had increased so much that the Van Caneghems decided to also begin collecting other, more affordable cars. The cars were mainly sourced from France, where they didn't fear armed farmers when hunting for cars.

By the '60s, the car collection had grown so vast that they needed a new building. So the Van Caneghem family built a new repair shop in Oosterzele, near

The collection's proprietor doesn't mind when enthusiasts walk through and lean over the cars, because it means he doesn't have to dust them off as often. PIETER RYCKAERT

What began after World War II as an auto repair shop with a small collection of Peugeots in an adjacent hanger has grown into an obsession that includes numerous vintage marques. PIETER RYCKAERT

Ghent, attached to a hangar that housed their collection, which by now numbered about 75 cars.

The garage was named Saint Martinus (Saint Martin) after a French saint renowned for donating his coat to a homeless man. And it is in this garage and adjacent hangar that the collection still resides today, long after Roger's father's passing.

Like the coat of Saint Martinus, the hangar protects the previously homeless cars from the elements. Some are in working order, but most haven't moved for decades. Predominantly Peugeots, brands such as Chenard & Walker, Renault, Austin, Imperia, Rolls Royce, Daimler, even Chevrolet and Buick can also be found. And the amount of parts and enamel signs on display is absolutely stunning.

Roger Van Caneghem doesn't suffer fools lightly but welcomes anyone with even a little bit of automotive passion into his sanctuary. "As long as people come and snoop around the cars, I don't have to take off all the cobwebs myself, you see," Roger says.

This collection was never intended to be commercially lucrative, but at the age of 75, Roger has started selling off cars. His children don't share his passion, and his hands and fingers have lost all feeling for nuts and bolts.

"Also, I've had some health problems lately, and once you get taken away in an ambulance, you start to look at life with different eyes," he says. "I have expressed my wish to an undertaker that I'd like to be buried with all my cars. But he said that might be a tad bit difficult, so I'll have a prayer with Saint Martinus to see if he can have a word with the Big Man upstairs."

CHAPTER 2

The Mail-Order Galaxie

Franklin Rechnitzer is no newcomer to discovering cars in his native Costa Rica. He has actually been featured in my previous book, *The Hemi in the Barn*, with a terrific Alfa Romeo Spider 2000 in rough condition that his uncle had stored in a garage, promising never to sell. When his uncle passed away, his wife immediately sold it to Rechnitzer.

But that's another story. For this one, Rechnitzer had known about a certain 1963 Ford Galaxie convertible for at least 15 years, which *also* happened to be owned by a man who said he wouldn't sell. Even though this Ford was stored in a garage, it was essentially an indoor playground for a couple of rambunctious boys who drew on it with markers, removed emblems and trim, and generally ruined

what had been a pristine, rust-free car. "The boys even used the convertible top as a trampoline," Rechnitzer says. "It was badly ripped."

Eventually, knowing he collected old cars, the owner offered the car to Rechnitzer in order to get it away from the boys. "My wife didn't want me to have any more cars, so initially I said no," he says. "But he offered it to me for a very fair price, so I bought it."

Living in Costa Rica means finding and buying parts for American cars is often tough and expensive. Rechnitzer was on the lookout for sideview mirrors, trim, badges, radio knobs, and more—replacing many of the parts the boys had destroyed was the first priority. But modern commerce came to the rescue. Rechnitzer was able to find everything he needed on eBay!

It may appear to be a Ford Galaxie, but neighborhood kids confused it with being a playground. When Franklin Rechnitzer decided to restore the car, he had to undo many of those past sins.
FRANKLIN RECHNITZER

CHAPTER 3
Low-Mileage Mouse Hotel

For some enthusiasts, the ultimate barn-find is a Cobra (for me it was a 289); for others, it could be a Z28 Camaro or a Duesenberg. For John Forbes, of Denver, North Carolina, it has always been a Porsche 914/6.

Forbes is a well-known Porsche mechanic, restorer, and racer. He has worked exclusively on Porsches for 42 years, the duration of his entire working life. As a teenager, he cut his teeth on a 911 at a gas station in Cherry Hill, New Jersey. In 1971, he became a mechanic at a Porsche dealership, specializing in engines and transmissions. His first exposure to racing came when he worked on Mark Donohue's Penske IROC Porsche at the dealership in 1974.

This is what a 1970 Porsche 914/6 with 5,000 miles on it looks like after it's been stored for 36 years. Owner John Forbes believes it is the lowest mileage six-cylinder 914 in the world.
JOHN FORBES

The racing bug had bit, and Forbes was hooked.

He raced a series of six-cylinder 914 Porsches, occasionally beating factory pros such as Hurley Haywood and Bob Snodgrass from Brumos Porsche in Jacksonville, Florida. Eventually Forbes opened his own Porsche repair facility—Black Forest Racing—and moved it to Denver, North Carolina, where he works on all Porsches, but prefers 914s.

For this Porsche barn-find story, though, we also need to mention a second Porsche mechanic named Wolfgang Schmidt. Schmidt worked in a Porsche dealership in southern New Jersey, and ordered a brand new, 1970 Irish Green 914/6 with black interior, appearance group, and steel wheels. He used the car sparingly on weekends for three years when, tragically, he was stricken with muscular dystrophy in his mid-30s. In 1976, he passed away.

His grieving widow parked the low-mileage Porsche in the garage next to a VW Beetle, where it sat untouched from 1976 to 2012. It was about that time that Forbes received a phone call from a friend, Karl, who operated a VW repair shop in New Jersey.

"Karl told me one of his customers was 75 years old and was selling her house," Forbes says. "He told me she had an old 914 Porsche in the garage that she needed to sell. He asked if I was interested."

It wasn't even a choice. Forbes hooked up his trailer and made the 500-mile trip to inspect the car as soon as he could. What he discovered was an Irish Green "mouse hotel." Mice, and probably

This is the same 914 after removing lots of acorns and the mouse hotel, installing new rings, and doing a good compound and polish. JOHN FORBES

chipmunks, had taken residence in the car during its 36-year slumber.

"The gas in the tank had turned to mud and the interior smelled really bad," he says. "But the odometer showed a correct reading of only 5,020 miles."

He and friend Robert Fleischer bought the car, and finally Forbes realized his barn-find dream. "Acorns were everywhere—in the glove box, in the heater channels, and under the gas tank," he says. "But the original tires held air, and the carpets cleaned up nicely. Thankfully we were able to get the smell out."

Forbes removed the engine (which was stuck), cleaned it, and installed new rings. The dual Weber carbs only needed cleaning. The car was polished and displayed at several Concours d'Elegance events, winning the most original, lowest-mileage car at one.

Porsche connoisseur Bob Ingram, chairman of the Pinehurst Concours in North Carolina, paid Forbes the highest compliment.

"He told me this could be the lowest mileage 914/6 in the world," Forbes says.

Maybe the one most appreciated by rodents, too.

CHAPTER 4

Clapped-Out Mexican Lotus

When Bruce Gross bought the clapped-out Lotus Formula Junior from an El Paso backyard, he had no idea of the car's early history.

His first exposure to the car was in the mid-1970s, when he raced an MGB in an autocross event in the El Paso area. He was a Lotus enthusiast and couldn't help but take notice when an early Lotus 18 began showing up at the events. He was young, though, and could only afford to admire the car from a distance.

Later, Gross satisfied his Lotus lust in 1976 when he moved to California and bought an Elan. But five years later, he was back in El Paso and began racing again, haunted by thoughts of that Lotus 18. He needed to locate it. He looked up old SCCA event results from the mid-1970s and found the Lotus and the owner's name.

Turns out the owner had a local speed shop.

Gross visited the owner and found the car under a tarp in his backyard. They struck a deal, and Gross finally owned the car. What he didn't know, however, was that the car was one of five new ones that were

Originally shipped to Mexico to establish a Formula Junior class there, Bruce Gross's Lotus spent time as an autocrosser and even a drag racer! It's enough to make constructor Colin Chapman blush!
BRUCE GROSS

Here the Lotus is equipped with Zoomie headers and a Pinto overhead cam 2-liter instead of its original pushrod 1-liter engine. BRUCE GROSS

Gross ultimately traded his Lotus for a Formula Ford. The Lotus made its way back to England where it was restored and painted in the same color scheme as when it arrived in Mexico almost 60 years earlier. BRUCE GROSS

shipped from England to Mexico City in 1960 to establish the Formula Junior class in that country. The car finished eighth in the 1961 Mexican Grand Prix Formula Junior race with original owner Jose Luis Mulas behind the wheel. Mulas had ordered the car in light blue with red numbers to reflect his French heritage.

Later, the car bounced around between owners in Mexico, New Mexico, and Texas before being rebuilt, believe it or not, as a *drag racer* with metal-flake paint and zoomie headers. Eventually it became an autocross racer, which is the era when Gross first saw the car in the mid-1970s.

Gross bought the Lotus in 1981 and autocrossed it for the next nine years. "I was actually racing a Lotus," Gross says. "It was the same model that my hero Jimmy Clark started his Lotus racing career with in 1960."

When he sold it, even though he had modified it slightly, he was able to present the new owner with all the original parts he had saved, including the original Cosworth MK IV engine. "I didn't have the money to restore the car, so I advertised it in *Hemmings*," Gross says. "The ad said, 'Want to trade Lotus Formula Junior in need of restoration for restored Lotus Formula Ford.' I traded the car for a beautiful Lotus 51C, which allowed me to go vintage racing. It was British Racing Green with a yellow stripe and red interior."

The car ultimately found its way back to England, where it was restored to the condition and colors it wore in the 1961 Mexican Formula Junior race. Since then, the car has been raced and displayed throughout the United Kingdom at vintage events.

"For me," Gross says, "the ultimate Lotus freak, to find and buy that car was my ultimate goal."

II

PHD BARN-FINDERS

CHAPTER 5
The Hidden Holman-Moody

Even the most dedicated car restorer would probably have ignored the rusty hulk that John Craft discovered in a Virginia field.

It was obviously some sort of stock car—probably 1960s vintage—but it was so badly rusted that it would have been a shame to halt the ashes-to-ashes, dust-to-dust cycle it had begun.

But to Craft, a PhD, lawyer, and professor (but mostly a renowned stock car racing historian and author), he had just stumbled upon a piece of gold. Craft specializes in vintage Ford stock cars built by Holman-Moody. He had already found and restored a couple of Holman-Moody cars.

"This car was dumb luck," the Texas resident says.

"I never thought I'd find another Holman-Moody car."

How Craft came to know of this car was a fluke. "I was on a scale car model builders' forum," he says. "And someone started a thread: 'Wonder whatever happened to all the old cars?' Then another guy sent in two photos: one of a car in a field, and the other of the Holman-Moody ID plate."

It was a 1964 Galaxie, originally manufactured at Ford's Norfolk, Virginia, assembly plant. The "roller" was delivered to Holman-Moody in Charlotte, complete with interior and windows but minus engine and transmission. The car was then converted to NASCAR racing specs at Holman-Moody and painted George Barris Candy Apple Tangerine.

Once painted a brilliant shade of Candy Apple Tangerine, they don't deteriorate much worse than this. But historian Dr. John Craft saw the original Holman-Moody plaque and realized this car was worth saving. JOHN CRAFT

Most people seeing this would imagine Craft was taking the rusty stocker to the recycler. Instead, Craft was getting ready to roll up his sleeves and restore the significant racer. JOHN CRAFT

Hard work and elbow grease has turned the rusty hulk into this showpiece. Craft was able to retain parts of the chassis and lower control arms. JOHN CRAFT

The Galaxie was raced by Skip Hudson (Riverside), Bobby Marshman (Daytona 500), Augie Pabst (Sebring support race), and Larry Frank (Atlanta 500) in 1964. It was then sent north to race in USAC.

In 1965, it returned south and served as Jabe Thomas's NASCAR rookie ride. When Ned Jarrett lost his team car to a transport accident that season, Thomas rented the car to him at Nashville. Thomas used the car again during the 1966 Grand National season before it was put out to pasture.

"At the end of the 1966 season, Thomas brought the car to a field, stripped it, and there it sat for 41 years," Craft says. Craft asked the owner if he'd consider selling. The answer was yes, and a comprehensive restoration was begun.

"The chassis needed lots of work," he says. "I was able to salvage the frame, lower control arms, and pedals. It was rumored that H & M used 'chemical milling' and other lightening techniques to keep pace with the Hemis in 1964. That is possibly one reason the car was in such bad shape; that and Thomas wrecking a lot."

Using bodywork from a rust-free Arizona 1964 Galaxie, the restoration is nearly complete. The car was recently hand-lettered in the original Holman-Moody style by NASCAR archivist Buz McKim. When completed, Craft hopes to race the Ford in vintage stock car races at Sebring, Florida, and Laguna Seca, California.

An interesting note: Just before Craft purchased the Ford from the field, another stock car that had been resting next to it for many years was crushed. "It was Richard Petty's 1969 Plymouth Roadrunner," says Craft. "The only thing that saved this Ford from being crushed was the tree that had grown through the engine compartment."

CHAPTER 6
One Lucky John

Lucky John Craft. Through investigation, following up leads, and as he admits, dumb luck, he has discovered a number of authentic Ford stock cars built by the legendary Holman-Moody race team.

Certainly finding and restoring Fred Lorenzen's 1965-Daytona-500-winning Galaxie was the crowning jewel of his car-collecting career. But his recent discovery of a significant 1968 Ford Torino also ranks as the equivalent of striking gold among his circle of collectors.

Dr. John Craft is a lawyer in Texas. Prior to that, he was a police officer and a law school professor. With all these careers and degrees, it's a wonder that he has any time to collect and restore old racecars.

But restore them he does. Craft investigates his projects with academic fervor. When restoring a car, he performs his own welding, fabricating, and engine building. The good doctor does nearly everything except final paint.

Opposed to many of the vintage racecars he has discovered (which were wrecked, then scrapped), this

Rusty discoveries just seem to follow Dr. John Craft home. This hulk once powered Bobby Allison to a third-place finish in the 1968 Daytona 500. His plan is to restore this former Holman-Moody racer. JOHN CRAFT

1968 Torino had an easier retirement. "Its life was not ended by catastrophic wreck," he says. "It was simply raced, then parked."

Holman-Moody chassis number HM8-033S began as a 1967 #29 Ford Fairlane. It was owned by Bondi Long and driven by Dick Hutcherson. At the conclusion of the 1967 season, the car was sent back to Holman-Moody and rebodied as a 1968 Torino. As a Torino, the car was driven by Bobby Allison to a third-place finish in the 1968 Daytona 500 behind Cale Yarborough and Leroy Yarbrough.

That summer, A.J. Foyt drove the Torino in the Firecracker 400, Swede Savage drove the car at Rockingham, and "Little" Bud Moore raced the car during the last few races of the season.

The car was eventually painted metal-flake blue and raced as a Sportsman before being parked in the proverbial field. "Ted Thomas discovered the car in a field in Tennessee," Craft says. "Ted then sold car to Dale Sale.

"I first saw the car in his warehouse 20 years ago. It still had the original Holman-Moody ID plate attached to it."

Sale accepted Craft's offer in 2008, when the country's economy was beginning to sink. "I dragged the car back to Texas," Craft says, who would restore the car back to its 1968 Daytona 500 configuration.

So far, he has secured a rare Ford 427 Tunnel Port engine, a Bud Moore air cleaner, and "lots of parts from Smokey Yunick's garage."

"Even though there is evidence of the original gold, white and red paint, there is no usable sheetmetal," Craft says. "Leaves on the roof caused the roof to rust through."

Craft has purchased a second, rust-free Torino GT, which he will strip of its sheetmetal and ultimately attach to his restored chassis. But there is no doubt about Craft's intentions for the car after the restoration is completed.

"The car will be race ready," he says.

CHAPTER 7

In Search Of Something Special

by Dr. Geoff Hacker

What Rick D'Louhy and I find most rewarding is putting together lost cars with the individuals or families who created them. That drives us more than any other reward. Sometimes we're lucky to make the connection—and sometimes we're really lucky—as with the story of the Siebler Special.

We started looking for the Siebler by studying an ad sent to us by good friend from California named Erich Schultz. An ad with a photo for a car appeared for sale in the December 1959 issue of *Hot Rod* magazine. Photos make it easier to identify, of course, but based on descriptions, we usually do pretty well with text-based ads too. The car was being sold by

Geoff Hacker followed up a lead about an unusual sports car in California. Turns out it was a Siebler Special, exactly what Hacker had been researching. GEOFF HACKER

After purchasing the Siebler Special, Hacker and buddy Rick D'Louhy dragged the car across the country to his Florida home. His plan is to restore the car so the Siebler family can again see it.
GEOFF HACKER

"Dick Siebler" of Reseda, California, and for several years that's all we had to go on.

When researching handcrafted specials of the '50s, we must be choosy in what we pursue when there is little or no information, so in this case we didn't move forward beyond the information and photo we had. That is, until, Dennis Garyson of West Covina, California, contacted us.

Gary sent us photos of a car he found at a local body shop. It had been removed from behind a house where it had sat outside for more than 40 years. In fact, the black California license plate still showed the 1963 registration. To our amazement we found that virtually nothing had been removed from the car since that time; the handmade air cleaner was still in place, and the chain-drive steering was fully functional. Only the seats were missing, and the floor had deteriorated due to years in the sun.

So we were off and running on what we found. When researching people 40-plus years later, I consider them to be like "fish on a reef;" that is, most don't stray far from home. In this case, I located the

son and daughter of Dick Siebler, both still living in California, not far from where they grew up.

Siebler's daughter, Patricia, was excited that we had found the car her father built in 1955, and couldn't wait to see it. She thought of it as part of her family and remembered her father building it and later riding in it. Siebler was proud of his accomplishment and won several trophies with his Special.

In the summer of 2013, Rick D'Louhy—my partner in "Forgotten Fiberglass"—and I traveled from Florida to Los Angeles and spent a day with Patricia and her father's car discussing memories of her dad, the car, and their family. It was a special time for all of us—and one that has lit a fire under us to get the car restored and back to show the family as soon as possible.

Of course there are new things you learn during research like this, surprises and intrigue enough to make it a regular automotive thriller of the best sort. So does anyone want to help us find the second "special" Dick Siebler built in the 1960s? Rick and I are off again on another adventure!

CHAPTER 8

Leo Lyon's Cover Girl

by Dr. Geoff Hacker

R ick D'Louhy and I specialize in writing stories about locating handcrafted cars of the 1930s through the 1960s. The stories we uncover never fail to impress about a car owners, their dreams, perseverance, and fortitude. The fact that so many cars were actually finished back then astounds me to this day.

While many handcrafted cars built over the years may not be ones that we recognize for their design and quality, some were made with sound vision, a good plan, lock-tight precision, and involved all the right people. The Leo Lyons Custom "Merc" was one such car.

In 2013, I began looking for a piece of automotive history that could double as my daily driver; something special to drive around my home in Tampa, Florida. Every day I peruse a number of automotive websites—my favorite is H.A.M.B., or Hokey Ass Message Board, a companion website to *Jalopy Journal.*

I was directed there by Kustomrama, another website on custom cars, which had posted a car for sale on H.A.M.B.—the striking Leo Lyons Custom Merc. What's more, it was the cover car of the February, 1960 issue of *Custom Cars* magazine. The car was reasonably priced, in nice condition, but in need of a full restoration. With Rick's support, we purchased the car from now good friend Craig Hahn.

The radical Mercury was not hiding; instead, it had been posted on several Internet sites, but surprisingly only Hacker appeared interested in owning the car. GEOFF HACKER

Hacker purchased the Mercury custom, then showed it to original builder Leo Lyons, who built the car more than half a century earlier. GEOFF HACKER

And then our research started. Who was Leo Lyons, and what happened to him?

With little effort, I found Leo in his hometown of San Bernardino, California, and did he have a story to tell. He shared that the Merc took nine years in planning, design, and construction. When I asked him about the "donor car," he stopped right in his tracks.

"Donor car?" he asked. "There was no such thing—with Ford's support, I bought all parts for my car new, including the chassis!"

It turned out that Leo had struck a deal with Ford, which provided 10 sets of 1950 Mercury body panels that Leo and his entourage used to build 10 identical custom cars. I then asked who had helped him build his car, and learned another surprising fact. He said that his friends George and Sam—the Barris brothers, an early California customizing team—helped him perfect his craft. Sam, in particular, helped him learn how to lead and braise metal so that extensive modifications could be made throughout the body.

"Anybody else help?" I asked Leo again. "Yes," he said, "California Metal Shaping custom built and fit the hood, doors, and top."

After learning the significance of the car, Rick and I chose to ship it to the Los Angeles area and reunite Leo Lyons with his custom car—the first time he had seen it in nearly 50 years. Jay Leno sent his crew there to film the event, and we hope to share that video in the near future. In the meantime, restoration of the car began in late 2013, and we hope to have the car in show-ready shape by late 2014.

CHAPTER 9
Cinnamon Girl

by Dr. Geoff Hacker

R ick and I like to say that we specialize in finding cars that no one's looking for. And for the life of me, I can't understand why—there are so many cars with great stories out there that need saving, preserving, sharing, and celebrating that we need as many of us to save them as we can get. We can't do it alone.

Enter Tom Chandler, of Elkader, Iowa.

I've known Tom and his wife, Barb, for many years. We first met because of a mutual interest in rare and unusual cars. Tom and Barb own a beautifully restored 1952 Glasspar G2. The G2 is known as America's first fiberglass-bodied sports car—a car that debuted at the 1951 Petersen Motorama in Los Angeles, California. Tom called me several years ago about a car he had seen in the woods near the interstate for many years.

Tom thought it looked like a '53 Grantham Stardust—another low-production, hand-built car—but he couldn't get close enough to the car to confirm. What he did see, however, was *rust*. Since the Stardust was one of my fiberglass favorites, it couldn't be the same car, which even intrigued me more. As far as I know, fiberglass doesn't rust.

We're always researching many cars at once, and it took about six months before Tom was able to visit the closest farm where the car was seen. "Yes," they said, it was their car, but it was sold to another person

Cinnamon Girl sat on an Iowa farm field for many years. Only because it was visible from the road was it discovered. Makes you wonder how many cars are hiding that are not visible. GEOFF HACKER

in Iowa who had plans to restore it. Jerry Smith was the person whom Tom had met, and it was his father who had built the car, back in the late '50s.

Sometimes I'm pleased to know that a car I was interested in has been rescued by someone else. I liked the styling of this car—swoopy fenders, low stance, hand-built with steel—very cool. So I smiled to myself that the car was not lost but "found" by another enthusiast, and I looked forward to seeing the car (hopefully sometime in the near future) restored and being appreciated for its history, design, and heritage.

About a year later, I got an email from good friend Nick Whitlow. "Geoff . . . did you see the car on the H.A.M.B. for sale," he wrote.

Of course, it was the car from Iowa, now for sale and at a very reasonable price.

Geoff Hacker proudly stands next to what he calls his Cinnamon Girl, or the Smith Six, which was built from steel by Duane Smith in 1959. GEOFF HACKER

I beat feet and contacted the owner. I spent more money shipping the car back to Tampa than I had paid for the car itself. The body, though rusty, turned out to be mostly surface rust. The frame was another matter, but we're in the process of securing another Henry J frame to put underneath it and make it right as rain again.

When Duane Smith finished his car in 1959, it was the culmination of three years of work. Rightly so, he named his car the "Smith Six," wherein "Six" designated the number of cylinders. I have come to affectionately call it "Cinnamon Girl" due to its rust hue having been seasoned in the elements for nearly 40 years and for my appreciation of Neil Young and his song by the same name.

CHAPTER 10
The 1954 Chicagoan: The Second Time's The Charm

by Dr. Geoff Hacker

As Rick D'Louhy and I began our quest to document low-production, handcrafted fiberglass cars from the 1950s, I was intrigued by a car called the "Chicagoan" that appeared in literature at the time. Chicago is my home town, or at least now the home town of my parents. They have reminded me over the years that I grew up in the *suburbs* of Chicago, while *they* were true "Chicagoans."

Oh well. I thought it was a car worthy of study, and off I went on a quest to find the people who were responsible for building it. From the scant material available, a company called Triplex was involved, as well as a company called Ketcham, both located on the south side of Chicago.

So I started out with the easiest way I knew how—look in the phone book. And while there was no "Ketcham" listed, there was a "Triplex" located mere

After much research, Geoff Hacker discovered that three Chicagoan sports cars were manufactured in 1954, a cooperative project between three Chicago-based companies. GEOFF HACKER COLLECTION

Of the three cars built, Hacker has located two and owns this one. It is currently under restoration and will debut at the 2015 Chicago Automobile Show, 61 years after it was manufactured. GEOFF HACKER

Hacker commissioned this gorgeous rendering to show how his Chicagoan should look when restored. GEOFF HACKER

blocks away from the original location of where the car was produced. On closer inspection, the Triplex company had worked with automotive products since the '50s, and they reproduced plastic parts for various manufacturers.

"Man, this research thing is easy," I thought to myself. I called the company and arranged a conference call with the owner, the son of whom founded the organization. And while he was quite helpful and even interested, he assured me they never produced a car or body or anything like that. He was fascinated that a project such as the "Chicagoan" was produced near him, but he claimed to never have heard of it.

In times like this, research begins to feel not so easy.

So I took a deep breath and considered that maybe it was a "skunkworks," or secret project that the son never knew about. I contacted the Chicago Historical Association to learn more about the people who were officially tied to the company in 1953 and 1954, hoping that a lead would follow. It did not, and I was perplexed—most of the research we've done has resulted in finding the families and even individuals who produced the cars we've sought. This project seemed easy at first but quickly came to a dead end.

What's a car guy to do? I took a page from Sherlock Holmes, who said, "When you have eliminated the impossible, whatever remains, however improbable, must be the truth." I called the Chicago Historical Society back and asked, "Were there any other companies in Chicago called Triplex back in the '50s?"

"Yes," they replied, and they provided the names and addresses relevant to the company from the 1950s. One or two phone calls later, I was on the phone with Steve and Sharon Hinger. Steve's father, Frank Hinger, was the owner of Triplex back then, and indeed it was an entirely separate company located just blocks away from the other Triplex company still in business.

It turns out that Frank hired Robert Owens to design the car for his company, Triplex Industries. Then Triplex contracted with Ketcham's Automotive Corporation nearby to distribute completed cars and kits to build the car. The Chicagoan project was also sponsored by U.S. Gymsum, and all involved produced the car to debut at the 1954 Chicago Auto Show, which it did in grand style. Three factory cars were made, and subsequently all disappeared after the show.

To date, I've found two Chicagoans and own one of them. My Chicagoan is currently in restoration, and I hope to showcase the restored car at the 2015 Chicago Auto show—61 years after its original debut in 1954.

CHAPTER 11
The Last, Fast Singer

by Dr. Geoff Hacker

I think of Rick D'Louhy and myself as champions of the forgotten—cars and people who accomplished amazing things when the skills, resources, and money needed to accomplish such endeavors were often few and far between.

During the 1950s, building your own sports car was often a viable and necessary step toward ownership when most of what was out there was from overseas. And getting an edge on the competition meant increasing speed, magnifying horsepower, dropping weight, and other secrets, some of which have been lost to time.

One of the ways that some enterprising young Americans could have their cake and eat it too was to rebody a foreign sports car, often an MG or other such car. One of the cars that were rebodied at the time was a car called a "Singer" from the United Kingdom.

Not many were done, though, and most were just built as a one-of-one, ultra-limited edition, and the best known of these cars on a Singer frame with drivetrain was designed, built, and sold by Kjell Qvale and his BMC Corporation based in San Francisco. Kjell Qvale made a few bodies, sports cars, and racecars using Singers, and we're still on the lookout for an example (and we think we're close to finding our first one). Jules "Jay" Heumann, chairman emeritus of the Pebble Beach Concours d'Elegance, also built a one-off Singer special.

Geoff Hacker became intrigued with racing Singer automobiles. Here is Ralph Bush racing his Singer at the Pomona race course in the early 1950s. GEOFF HACKER COLLECTION

In the process of researching Singer-derived specials, Hacker happened upon this 1952 Singer, the last racing Singer. Hacker (right) is posing with the car's original builder/racer Ralph Bush. GEOFF HACKER

So by the time we had finished researching as many (if not most and probably all) of the Singer specials built in the 1950s, I had become good friends with Peter McKercher, vice president of the North American Singer Owners Club. One day, Peter announced that with all the research I had completed on Singer specials of the '50s I was now one of two historical Singer experts in North America.

Wow! I was honored, so I asked Peter if I shouldn't go ahead and find an interesting Singer out there to save, restore, and show. "Was there anything interesting?" I asked him. And he began to tell me about the story about Ralph Bush and the Last Racing Singer.

Ralph was a member of the Singer Owners Club back then, and was racing Singers in the early '50s with other members. In late '50s, he decided he wanted to race a Singer again, and he purchased one from a friend. By 1960, he was racing at such tracks as Pomona, Riverside, Santa Maria, Santa Barbara, Taft, Las Vegas, and other such venues. Several years later he decided to sell his car, and he never saw it again.

Never saw it, that is, until it appeared on Tam's Old Race Car Site (http://www.tamsoldracecarsite.net/). Eric Weese had decided to sell cars that had been in his father's collection (the James Weese Collection),

and while many had been sold, this one remained. In fact, it had been for sale for two to three years in plain sight on the website at a very reasonable price.

The perfect car for me! With Tam McPartland's help, I contacted Eric and made arrangements to purchase the car. But before shipping it home to Tampa, we found Ralph Bush and invited him to join us to celebrate his car and his memories of it at my friend Erich Schultz's home in Pasadena, California, before shipping it home.

Much to our great pleasure, Ralph accepted the offer. He joined us in the summer of 2013 for the visit, reuniting with his old car. We spent the day having a great time reliving his memories. We even did two short videos of this event, and they're available on YouTube for the world to see.

So I now have a racecar—a 1952 Singer 4AD—with great history and in need of great restoration. What makes this even more amazing for me is that it's the only known Singer car with racing history that has ever been found here in the States. It's quite an honor for me to have stewardship of this car and its history, and I hope to be able to bring this car and its story back to prominence and make all those involved—especially Ralph Bush—proud in every way.

CHAPTER 12
Junkyard Girls Are The Best

by Dr. Geoff Hacker

A lost car found in a junkyard? Covered in snow? What's the car? Where is the junkyard? How did it get there? I love those kinds of questions!

I've been on the hunt for a McCormack sports/custom car since first seeing one in 2006 in Texas. Rick D'Louhy and I didn't pounce quickly enough, though, and we lost the car to a now good friend in Australia. Were there any McCormacks left in the USA? I was hopeful that there were, and I was bound and determined to find one.

Around 2010, I began receiving emails of a mysterious car in a junkyard somewhere in the northeast—the hunt was on. When I finally found the link to the car on the Internet, it turned out to be a video of a lost junkyard, and the video was even set to music. The video was artistic and featured beautiful cars in the snow. And there it was—another McCormack! I had to find out where the junkyard was and learn its history, too.

It took about a year, but I tracked down the source of the video—Marc Reed. Marc agreed to help me

While researching the McCormack sports car, Geoff Hacker heard about a possible example in a Pennsylvania junkyard. He discovered and purchased this relic, which had been drag raced at one time.
GEOFF HACKER

What's New in the 1956 Cars

MOTOR Life | FORD V-8 Road Test

February 25¢

The Latest in Custom Styling

Geoff Hacker often starts with a vintage magazine cover or story about a homebuilt special. This *Motor Life* cover shows a concept rendering of the McCormack sports car. GEOFF HACKER

on my quest and provided information about the junkyard, but it appeared to be abandoned. With a bit more help from local sources, I tracked the car down to a small yard in New Hope, Pennsylvania, a town known for its quaint antique shops, not its fantastic junkyards. I was getting close!

I made a few more calls, and I was soon in touch with Bob Truitt and his mother, Doris—great folks in every way. Bob had acquired the car years earlier

from his friend Graham Orton. A few more calls, and Graham and I were speaking. He shared that he had found the car in New Jersey many years before and that it had a great engine in it at one time. The owner he bought it from had bought the car for the engine and pushed the car out back, abandoning it for years.

During several conversations with current owner Bob Truitt, I put together a deal and made arrangements to save the car. At Christmas time in 2011, I hitched my trailer to my Suburban, filled it with gas, and headed north, and just days before Christmas, I had my new acquisition in hand—a 1955 (or so) McCormack.

I motored back home and began to research again too. So far, we've determined that the car raced at ATCO Dragway (New Jersey) in the '60s or '70s. It was painted green, just like how it appeared on the cover of *Motor Life* back in 1956, but it was clearly not the original cover car. This was a car built for speed. The entire frame was round tube and well built in every way. We've been working with drag racing historian and photographer Bob Wenzelburger to identify the original owner and builder, but the question still remains open at this time.

Our hope is to restore this car back to its original racing beauty. And if luck, time, and money allows, install a Dodge (long) cross ram engine underneath its extremely wide hood. The space is there, and it would be a remarkable way to show a car, its history, and potential to all interested. And perhaps by then we may have the rest of the story, as Paul Harvey used to say.

HIDING IN PLAIN SIGHT

CHAPTER 13
Ghost Of A Moonshine Runner

Michael Cummings did not discover his Ford coupe; he bought it from the guy who found it. But when he had first seen it advertised in *Hemmings Motor News*, he had to have it.

When Cummings, of Cumming (what a coincidence!), Georgia, was stuck in the Atlanta airport with a delayed flight, he needed a way to pass a few hours. So he went to the magazine store and bought a copy of *Hemmings Motor News*, sat in the gate area, opened the pages, and dreamed away his layover. And though he had always wanted a 1940 Ford, a certain 1939 model jumped off the page.

Even though the car was a 1939 with windshield

Rocket Power! When police cars began to catch up with the flathead V-8 engines, many moonshiners installed this hot, new power plant: the Oldsmobile overhead valve Rocket 88 engine! MICHAEL CUMMINGS

wipers *above* the windshield, it resembled a 1940 Ford, replete with Deluxe front and rear fenders, grill, dashboard, and title. What really got Cummings's attention, though, was the mention of two items: "Oldsmobile engine," and "moonshine runner." The car reminded Cummings of the racing coupes that ruled the Modified stock car circuit when he watched as a kid at small racetrack near his upstate New York home.

If this coupe could talk, imagine the stories it would tell about hauling loads of mason jars filled with white lightning and being chased by revenuers through the back roads of South Carolina and Georgia! Ford coupes, especially 1940 models, were particularly sought after by early moonshiners because the cars were light, the trunks were large enough to haul liquor, and the flathead V-8 engines were easily modified with dual carburetors and high-compression aluminum heads. But when overhead-valve Oldsmobile and Cadillac engines were introduced in the early 1950s, the bar was raised as those huge engines were installed in the small coupes.

The same cars that had transported illegal liquor during the week were often raced on weekends on bull-ring dirt tracks carved out of a farmer's field. They led dual lives, just like their drivers.

"I had just read the book, *Driving with the Devil*, and I had always been interested in 1940 Fords," says Cummings, who is the principle of a motorsport financing business. "Apparently this coupe was used

Michael Cummings found this former moonshine-running 1939/40 Ford coupe in *Hemmings Motor News*. The car is rough, but his plans are to keep the cosmetics as-is and restore it mechanically. MICHAEL CUMMINGS

to run liquor until about 1969, when the moonshiner bought an El Camino to replace it."

Back in the day, the owner of the coupe installed a 303 cubic-inch Oldsmobile "Rocket" engine, which was the engine swap of choice among moonshine runners in that era. The engine is adapted to the stock 1939 Ford three-speed floor shift gearbox.

The coupe's body has seen better days. And even though it is straight, the rain gutters are badly deteriorated. What's more, the floor is rusted where mice relieved themselves over the years, succumbing to the kind of natural erosion old and abandoned cars suffer.

Cummings did some investigating, though, and discovered that the car had spent much of its life running shine in South Carolina before moving south to Georgia in 2011.

"I think I'm going to keep it looking like it does, and totally restore it mechanically," he says. "I'd like to bring it to the annual Dawsonville (Georgia) Moonshine Festival, where there is always a huge selection of 1940 Fords."

As to whether or not that field of Fords carries illegal moonshine in their trunks, Cummings will just have to wait and see.

CHAPTER 14
You Can Find Anything Online

It was a posting on Craigslist.com that got Lars Ekberg's attention—a 1969 Ford Torino Talladega located in Clemson, South Carolina, just a few hours away from his North Carolina home.

Talladegas are rare cars, built to homologate the body for NASCAR competition. Traditionally, NASCAR required that at least 500 be built for street use in order to race on the track.

"I drove down and saw that the car wasn't worth what they were asking," Ekberg says. "So I made an offer, got in my truck, and drove home."

He never expected to hear from the owner again, but to his surprise, his phone rang about six months later. "The guy called and said to drive back down the next week, and to bring a winch," he says.

"He had accepted my offer." The former owners, a married couple, had owned the car for 20 or 25 years, according to Ekberg. The lady had tears in her eyes as he loaded the car on his trailer.

It had a 428 cubic-inch engine with a column shift automatic, but it was missing many parts under the hood. Luckily, when he opened the trunk, he discovered all the missing parts. "I brought the car home on a Friday night and had it running by Saturday morning," he says.

He enjoyed driving his barn-find to local cruise-ins for a couple of years, but eventually decided to move on to something else. "I sold it on eBay to a guy in California," Ekberg says.

Apparently someone needed that car more than Ekberg, and the price, once more, was right.

Surprisingly Lars Ekberg located this rare Torino Talladega on Craigslist. The car was built in small numbers, with the assistance of Charlotte's Holman-Moody, in order to make it legal for NASCAR competition. LARS EKBERG

It's all in the nose. This is the magic part that made the car so successful on the race track. The fenders and hood are several inches longer than stock, which gave it superior aerodynamics. LARS EKBERG

CHAPTER 15
A Kitten In The Classifieds

It's a good thing Hector Castro has friends.

Castro, who owns the renowned HRC Jaguars restoration shop, doesn't live in Chicago, but instead he resides in Denver, North Carolina. But when he answered the phone four years ago, a friend of his in Chicago was on the other end and had called to advise him that a pair of old Jaguars had just appeared in his local newspaper that morning.

"It was for two 1935 SS Airline Coupes, which were very limited production," Castro says. "Bill Harrah had one in his museum a long time ago. So I called and spoke to the owner for a while, and agreed to buy the two cars sight-unseen."

Castro says the model is extremely rare, and that probably no more than 10 remain in the world today out of 624 built between 1934 and 1936. The Airline Coupe differs from a standard version because the rear of the body is sloped down with a seductive curve in a streamlined, Art Deco style. The cars featured all-steel bodies built over sturdy wooden frames. Inside, occupants cuddled in four separate bucket seats.

Looking like a pile of so many car parts, actually two disassembled SS, or Jaguar, Airline Coupes are mixed up with other Jaguar parts. Hector Castro will assemble one or both of the gorgeous cars, but his waiting list is years long. TOM COTTER

The cars were powered by 2.5 liter push-rod engines that breathed through two SU carburetors, generating 70 horsepower. They were capable of achieving about 100 miles per hour.

The two cars Castro purchased have a particularly interesting and tragic story. Originally imported from New Zealand to California, they were purchased by two friends, a doctor and a restorer. Their plan was for the doctor to fund the two cars' restoration, which would be performed by his partner, the restorer. They would then sell the cars and split the profits.

Both cars were assembled and complete when purchased by the two gentlemen. But when the restoration began, the cars were disassembled nut-by-nut, bolt-by-bolt. Then, tragically, the restorer/partner died, and the doctor was stuck with two rare, albeit disassembled Jags. He was not in a position to complete the projects and was forced to sell them at fire-sale prices.

"So this guy in Chicago bought them, thinking he could restore and sell the cars," Castro says. "But it was too big a project for him, so that's when they were advertised in the Chicago newspaper."

Castro purchased the cars on behalf of a client, and they are in line to become restored, although he has a five-year waiting list. "At this point, I'm not sure if I'll restore both cars or just one and use the second car for parts," Castro says.

Today, the two cars sit literally in a pile of what appear to be rusty, generic old car parts in the corner of the HRC shop in North Carolina—a sad fate for two gorgeous cars.

But Castro has a reputation of taking rusty, old, generic car parts and making beautiful machinery out them.

CHAPTER 16
A Rare And Exquisite Beauty

Brian Laine likes quirky cars. At the top of the food chain in his garage in Arlington, Washington, Laine has an original 427 Cobra. At the bottom, he has a recently restored Pedi-Cab. In between, he has a Sunbeam Tiger, Morris Minor Traveler woody, a Bug Eye Sprite, and a V-8-powered Datsun 240 Z.

So when he saw a 1933 MG J-2 pop up on Craigslist.com, he called right away. The MG also appeared on Bring-A-Trailer.com, which made it very popular to a worldwide audience.

"The seller suddenly had offers for the car much higher than his advertised price," Laine says. "But he did an online search on me and saw I owned a Cobra. 'Oh, I see you own a Cobra,' said the advertiser," Laine says. "I guess that broke the ice for me, because he sold the car to me. He was a good man."

Laine thinks the seller believed that if he had the wherewithal to own a Cobra, he certainly had enough money to restore the MG to a high standard. And he wasn't about to say anything to make the seller believe otherwise.

Laine hooked up his trailer and headed toward Seattle, where the car was located. The wheels didn't roll, so it needed to be dragged onto the trailer.

Now the quandary was to restore or not to restore? The engine in the car is incorrect, as are many other critical parts. The original overhead cam engine is very rare and not readily available. Besides, it only had two main bearings, causing the crankshafts to break easily.

To hot rod or to restore, now *that* is the question. "I'm in a quandary," Laine says. "But I just bought a little V-8 '60. . . ."

Brian Laine is always searching for interesting British vehicles. This rare MG showed up on Craigslist. He decided not to restore it; instead, he installed a Ford V-8 60 Flathead.

IV

WHEN NO MEANS YES

CHAPTER 17

Persistence Is Key

In a primal way, the sign on the windshield said it all: "No Sale," in much the same way a caveman might say "want eat!" or "fire hot!" The owner of the 1946 Chevrolet pickup truck was simply tired of every other car passing his home in China Grove, North Carolina, and stopping to inquire if it was for sale.

Meanwhile, Dan Wampler, just 20 miles away in Concord, was looking for a Chevy truck just like this one.

"I'm partial to trucks and told friends to keep their eyes open for something interesting," Wampler says. At 60 years old, he's been looking for something interesting for quite some time. "I had been picking up this part and that part for years, just waiting for the right truck to put them on."

One day Wampler mentioned to his next-door neighbor, Earl, he was on the lookout for a 1946 or '47 Chevy truck as a project. "Earl said his brother-in-law had one like that next to his house," Wampler says.

The truck had been pushed out of the shed when it started to fall down, so it sat for years just 15 feet from the road. And even though it wasn't "For Sale," Dan Wampler was able to purchase it.
DAN WAMPLER

Wampler is in the process of modernizing the mechanics of this truck but decided to leave the body and paint in its natural "patina." DAN WAMPLER

You guessed it—it turned out to be the "No Sale" truck in nearby China Grove, and because Wampler was introduced by Earl, he wasn't immediately chased off the property. "It had been stored in a shed, but when it started to fall down, the owner pushed it out of the shed so it wouldn't get damaged," he says. "It sat just 15 feet off from the road! He bought it in 1970 and was just tired of people stopping."

Wampler had a good conversation with the truck's owner, who probably realized he would never fix it up the way he had hoped 28 years earlier. The owner complained that purchasing parts was difficult, and besides, he admitted that he was actually a Ford guy.

"I told him if he sold it to me, I wouldn't chop it all up," Wampler says. "I told him I would keep the patina just like it was on the body, and just clearcoat the old paint and rust. He came up with a price and I bought it right there." When Wampler dragged the truck home, he was pleased to discover the original six-cylinder engine had been replaced with a newer 1958–1962 235 cubic-inch version.

Since he began working on the truck, Wampler has been a busy. He works at Keith Irwin Restorations, one of the area's hot rod shops, so he works on other people's hot rods during the day and tinkers with his own at night. "The 235 engine runs great," he says. "I found a rebuilding tag on it, so it's probably fairly fresh."

So far, he has installed a Fatman Mustang II front end, Chevy S-10 five-speed transmission, 10-bolt, disc brake rear end, and SS Rally Wheels. "I'm a big fan of Rally Wheels," Wampler adds. "I have them on all my cars and trucks."

He and wife, Tammy, plan to use the truck as a daily driver. Tammy is an antique picker and hauls lots of old treasures back and forth to her antique store in Concord.

"It's going to look old on the outside, but be all late model underneath, because chrome don't get you home," Wampler jokes.

CHAPTER 18
Aunt Kiki's Irresistable Allure

I couldn't have been more than five years old, maybe six, when I got a ride in my first sports car. It was white, with a black hardtop, red interior, and had a stick shift. I can still see it in my mind's eye, more than half a century later.

The car belonged to a friend of my Aunt Kiki, and it may, in fact, have helped turn me into a lifelong sports car freak.

The car was a Mercedes-Benz 190 SL, and as opposed to some in the collector car world today, I *do* consider this a sports car. I love the way these cars look—the voluptuous curves of the fenders, the tail-lights, and the front grille. And I love its raspy little exhaust note.

There is something just so correct about a 190 SL's proportions. Soon after my ride in the Mercedes, my dad bought me a Dinky Toy of the same car, and I was smitten for life.

Years went by, and in that time, I'd owned nearly every sports car made: MGTD, MGB, MG Midget, Triumph Spitfire, Porsche 356, Porsche Carrera S, Corvette Sting Ray, Sunbeam Tiger, AC Cobra, Datsun 240 Z, even a Cunningham C3, and many others. I loved them all. But there was always a void in my automotive bucket list.

Until a few months ago.

My passion since I was about 14 years old has been to discover barn-find cars, the kind hidden away in barns, warehouses, garages, fields, and the ones forgotten altogether. I've written a number of books about the subject, and I'm always on the prowl for old cars and motorcycles as subjects for my next book.

Last fall, I was in Maggie Valley, North Carolina, where I heard an urban legend: a guy named Steve Davis supposedly had hundreds of old cars, and

Having been driven and parked inside a metal building 20 years earlier, I was lucky enough to negotiate the purchase of this Mercedes 190 SL. It is similar to the very first sports car I rode in as a kindergartener. TOM COTTER

The car was mechanically sound, but it now requires much metal work because of rust cancer. Luckily the purchase included all the metal repair panels. It is now undergoing restoration.
TOM COTTER

thousands of old motorcycles. It sounded like a dream come true, and I had to visit.

Steve was a heck of a nice fellow, and told me he had been picking and collecting since he was a kid. He also told me he didn't usually sell anything, but he'd be glad to show me his fields and barns stocked with old cars—Fords, Studebakers, many old Jaguars, MGs, Volvos, and more. But in one of his buildings, stored in a nice, dry corner, was a car that caught my attention: a dusty 190 SL.

Steve told me it was a 1955, and that he had last driven it over 20 years ago. I said I'd be interested in buying it if he'd part with it, and he said yes, but only if I gave him signed copies of each of my books.

No brainer. He named his price, and we shook hands on it.

Later, a friend of Steve's named Eugene Smyre picked up the car and is now restoring it for me. Eugene is no newcomer to the area of restoration, having restored, among others, the Mormon Meteor that won best of show at Pebble Beach and Amelia Island a few years ago.

So here I am, at 59 years old, about to be spiritually reunited with a car that turned me into a sports car junkie so long ago. I imagine the ride will be just as memorable!

V

FROM THE WRONG SIDE OF THE TRACKS

CHAPTER 19

The "Hotted-Up" Jabro

Is it a dance? A new type of chocolate candy? Actually, you'd need to be a real vintage sports car junkie to know that a Jabro was a small, American-built sports racer from the 1950s.

First of all, it's pronounced *jA-bro*, a combination of the first few letters of builder James Broadwell's first and last name. The car is an odd assembly of parts (common in the 1950s) put together to compete in sports car races against the more expensive, "proper" sports cars of the day.

Broadwell conceived the car to compete in the Sports Car Club of America's H-Modified class of small engine racecars. Broadwell purchased a 1949 Crosley and used its drivetrain to power his design, which he carved in scale from a block of wood.

Broadwell's space frame, which was styled after a Jaguar C-Type, was actually constructed from 1¼-inch television antennae tubing and weighed just 49 pounds. His "hotted-up" Crosley engine was capable of revving to 8,500 rpm, and he was very successful with the car on the track, taking trophies in a number of races.

Broadwell's concept of a lightweight racecar spurred a small business of producing bodies and chassis, allowing the customer to provide his own drivetrain.

Enter Paul Wilson. Paul doesn't know which drivetrain originally powered the Jabro he found

When Paul Wilson first saw the Jabro behind Oliver Kuttner's dealership, it looked like this; basically just a fiberglass body. The small, lightweight cars were usually powered by Crosley, SAAB, and even outboard boat engines. PAUL WILSON

Now restored and raced frequently, Wilson's Jabro is powered by a BMC Sprite drivetrain. Here it is racing in the Pittsburgh Vintage Grand Prix. PAUL WILSON COLLECTION

sitting behind a building in Virginia, not far from his home in Fairfield. "I bought it from Oliver Kuttner, a dealer who traded sports cars and racecars in the 1980s," Wilson says. "He had all sorts of stuff—even wrecked Maseratis—sitting behind his dealership. Just a bunch of old, interesting stuff."

That's usually the best kind of *stuff* to be found. And that's where Wilson found the Jabro body. As he remembers, he paid a "couple of hundred dollars" for it in 1993, and took two years to rebuild it. "What I wanted was a miniature version of all the cars I had admired my whole life," he says. "These cars were an interesting hodge-podge of parts and powered by Crosley, Saab, and even Mercury Outboard engines."

Wilson began constructing a new chassis for the car, one that would both be safer than the original but also accommodate his more than 6-foot-tall frame.

He decided to use Austin Healey Sprite components, including wire wheels and a 1275 cc drivetrain.

"According to legend, Broadwell's buddies welded the frames in his basement and were paid with all-you-can-drink beer," Wilson says. "I have no direct confirmation, but the welds suggest the story may be true."

He met with a professional chassis designer who educated him about calculating length, suspension pick-up points, and spring rates. "It was the most informative three hours of my life," Wilson says. The result was a Jabro-styled chassis midsection, but with modified front and rear sections.

Wilson races his Jabro at several vintage events each year at tracks like Virginia International Raceway and Summit Point (West Virginia) since unearthing the unique car more than 20 years ago.

CHAPTER 20
One Wild Ride

George Alderman has been a road racer for most of his life. Alderman is known for racing Datsun 240Zs and 510 sedans, because he was a Datsun dealer for many years in Wilmington, Delaware.

More recently, he has sold Lotus Caterham 7s, but when he was racing in the mid-1960s, just before Datsun and Lotus entered his vocabulary, Alderman raced an early Mustang in the SCCA Trans Am series. Alderman and racing buddy Brett Lunger were also itching to race at the Sebring Trans Am in 1966, but neither owned a car that was eligible.

"So we decided, 'Let's go,'" Alderman says, now 79 years old. They located a 1965 Mustang coupe that had been raced in SCCA's A-Production category by Buzz Marcus at Watkins Glen, New York, and Reading, Pennsylvania. "So I called Buzz and we bought the car from him."

The '65 coupe came off the Ford assembly line equipped with a plain-Jane six-cylinder, but within a year, the previous owner (Marcus) had car builder Ray Heppenstall install a HiPo 289 engine, Cobra aluminum-case T-10 four-speed gearbox, Cobra bucket seats, and a roll cage.

One of the first things Alderman and Lunger did to the Caspian Blue coupe was to paint it British Racing Green, probably because Alderman had raced so many British cars prior to the Mustang.

Almost 50 years ago, veteran driver George Alderman campaigned anything on four wheels, including this 1965 mustang Notchback, which he ran in the Trans-Am series and co-owned with Brett Lunger. The car had a Hi-Po 289 engine, Cobra transmission, gauges, and seats. GEORGE ALDERMAN

In January 2009, Alderman, his son, Paul, and restoration friend Erich Bollman repurchased the car. They intend to restore it to its 1967 Trans-Am livery and begin vintage-racing it.
GEORGE ALDERMAN

At the time of the 1967 Sebring Four-Hour race, Lunger was in the military and couldn't get leave, so Alderman drove the event solo and finished ninth overall. He also raced it at Marlboro, Maryland, and Reading, before selling the car in 1969 to local racer Norm Taylor.

By that time, his Datsun and Lotus franchises were cranking up, and he was mostly racing those brands. The Mustang was forgotten for 40 years until Alderman's son, Paul, began restoring and racing Mustangs. Paul began to ask his father where the old Mustang might be. He learned Taylor had stored the car in a lean-to building behind his water business.

"I called Norm [Taylor] and his wife about buying the car back, but they said no, and not to call back again," Alderman says. But Alderman knew one of Taylor's employees who confirmed that the car was still behind the building.

When Taylor died in 2008, one of his company's employees decided to clean up the work lot and towed a bunch of old trailers, an old Impala, and the Mustang to the dumps. "We had to race to the junkyard to retrieve it before it got crushed," Alderman says. Many of the car's racing parts were missing, such as the engine and the radiator.

"We were never able to inspect the trailers before they were crushed, and we believe the parts were in there," he says. But at least he got his old racer back.

Alderman, his son, Paul, and Erich Bollman—owner of Christiana Muscle Car Restorations, a partner in the car—are restoring it back to its Sebring race configuration in the hopes of racing it in a vintage series.

"It was such a wonderful car to drive," Alderman says. "I was always right up there with the Corvettes when I raced it in A-Sedan."

CHAPTER 21
Lo-Lo-Lo-Lo Lola

Hold on and pay attention, because this story moves fast, and I only have 500 words to get it right.

Paul Wilson (also featured elsewhere in this book) met Tom Pollock while in grad school at the University of Virginia, and a long friendship ensued.

As a kid growing up in Washington, D.C., Pollock fell in love with an odd-looking sports car that had languished in the streets for years. Finally, the neighborhood had had enough, and they sent the police to tell the owner to either move it or it would be junked.

Pollock heard of the ordeal and without really knowing what the car was, agreed to pay $1 and take it away. He was just 14 years old at the time.

Pollock dragged the car to his parent's house, where it sat in the driveway for years. He found out the car was actually a Peugeot Darl'Mat, one of six aluminum-bodied cars built to race at Le Mans in 1937 and 1938.

Pollock had partially disassembled the car, but was meticulous about identifying the parts. In 1977, when he graduated from the University of Virginia and accepted a job at Texas A&M, Pollock sold the car to Wilson for $1,200.

Wilson fiddled with the car, but realized over time that the car was becoming increasingly valuable. "I was convinced by people to not restore the car," Wilson says. "But I decided that it was not a car I

This is the car that started a series of great trades: a Peugeot Darl'Mat LeMans racer for which Paul Wilson's friend Tom Pollock paid only $1 to become owner. Wilson later bought the car from his friend for $1,200. PAUL WILSON

Not convinced the historic Peugeot was one he needed to own long-term, he traded it for this 1964 Ferrari Lusso. After several years of ownership and tired of only driving it on the street, Wilson traded the Lusso . . . PAUL WILSON

. . . for this 1966 Lola T-70 MKII. Now don't get excited; the Lola arrived in baskets and required much restoration before it looked this good. PAUL WILSON

really wanted to own. So in 1996, I traded it for a 1964 Ferrari Lusso."

Today, the Peugeot resides in Fred Simeone's incredible sports car museum in Philadelphia.

After seven years of Lusso ownership, Wilson decided he wanted a car he could race on the track rather than a Ferrari he could only drive on the street, so in 2003 he traded it for—get this—a 1965 Lola T-70 MK II. Granted, the car was disassembled and in need of total restoration, but Wilson was thrilled with his new acquisition.

"This Lola has a small-block Chevy engine," he says. "And it's one of the few vintage Can Am cars that retains its original chassis, wheels, suspension uprights, and transaxle."

Wilson's Lola was serial number #SL71/18, originally sold to South Carolina gentleman racer named Buck Fulp. Fulp raced the car in the USRRC when it was new in 1966. He won the Riverside and Watkins Glen races that year, and finished third at Mid-Ohio, but was eliminated from the championship after a freak eye injury and a broken shifter.

Wilson has owned the car for nine years, and took one year to complete its restoration.

Seeing Wilson pull the powerful Can Am Lola out of the small, enclosed trailer hitched to his Toyota pickup is a sight to behold. He now races the car a couple of times each year, alternating between it, his Elva, and his Jabro.

He said there is something special about driving this car, when compared to his four-cylinder racers. "It goes 165 down VIR's backstretch," he says. "And it's a sweetheart. Lola built an amazingly customer-friendly car."

So, get it? The $1 Peugeot begot a swap for a 1963 Ferrari Lusso, which begot a Lola Can Am car. Pretty amazing series of deals!

CHAPTER 22

The Sergeant Daughter's Rare Gift

Tony Giordano is a BMC freak. Case in point: this 1962 Austin Healey Sprite, #510 DWD. It was for sale in Texas, quite a long way from Giordano's Long Island home. He discovered it on Craigslist.com, and at first glance, it didn't seem too interesting—just another overpriced, dusty, dirty, and abused Sprite.

"They were asking $10,000," he says. "It looked more like a $500 car." But the more he looked at the photos and asked questions, the more intriguing the car became. "It had a very rare Warwick fiberglass hardtop, of which only three are known to remain," he says.

There was also a plaque on the dashboard that read: "Built especially for USAF Sergeant Rudolf A. Davila." Giordano bought the car from the daughter of Davila, its original owner, for half her original asking price.

The car also had a wood-rimmed steering wheel, wire wheels, and disc brakes, but it was the engine number that really grabbed Giordano's attention: XSP-1862-2. "It is extremely possible that this 995cc engine was in the 'Works' Le Mans Sprite, driven there by American John Colgate in 1961," he says.

"This car is one of one," he said. "There were two right-hand drives like it built, but this is the only left-hand drive."

So Long Island's Tony Giordano adds another rare racing BMC product to his stable: the only left-hand-drive, square body, Works-modified Sprite with a Le Mans racing engine. And once again, he stole it right from under the noses of thousands of other BMC enthusiasts on Craigslist.

There's a lesson here—when it comes to online sales, it's usually first come, first served!

The Austin-Healey Sprite #510DWD in this photo was purchased new by a U.S. Air Force Sergeant. This car was built with many rare racing parts, including a Sebring racing engine. TONY GIORDANO COLLECTION

Giordano discovered the car on Craigslist. It was generally ignored as an over-priced project car by enthusiasts; Giordano dug a little deeper and bought a rare piece of history. TONY GIORDANO

CHAPTER 23

Shelby's *Other* Racecar

Google the name Larry Nash, and you'll find a pretty impressive list of credentials: drag racing, Indianapolis 500, hot rods, big name drivers, and SCCA National Championships.

And listed there on the Nash Performance website, between Formula Atlantics and Motorola Cup, is Shelby Can Am (SCA). Don't feel bad if you don't know what Shelby Can Am is—the series only ran three years, from about 1993 to 1996. That's when Chrysler's money ran out.

The SCA class was developed by Carroll Shelby as an SCCA "Spec" class, which means that all the cars had to remain unmodified after delivery. Engines couldn't be opened, suspension points couldn't be relocated, and so on. The reason for this, of course,

was to determine who was actually the best driver, because all the cars are virtually identical.

"Carroll Shelby got a gift from Lee Iacocca to run the Dodge Shelby Pro Series for three years," says LeeAnne Nash, Larry's wife and former series director. "The series ran support races during CART, SCCA Trans Am, and NASCAR weekends."

The cars were fairly breathtaking to look at: the bodies were designed by Peter Brock and featured open wheels in the front and enclosed, skirted wheels in the rear. The cars were powered by 250-horsepower Dodge V-6 3.3 liter engines. They were powerful and light, equipped with a differential ratio that allowed the driver to break the rear tires loose at will!

Only 72 Shelby Can Am racers were built before the series stalled out in 1996, and not many remain

After a 60-day trash, Larry and LeeAnne Nash turned the one-time mongrel into a slick racer once again. Here the car is on its vintage racing debut in Sebring. BILL ABLE COLLECTION

When discovered in a race trailer after many years, the Shelby Can Am was a neglected and forgotten racer that had been put away wet. In its day, however, the car could break its wheels loose in top gear!
BILL ABLE COLLECTION

today. Nash believes that as many as 50 cars have been sold over the years to racers in South Africa, where they have been converted with new bodywork into a different class.

One of the early cars was purchased by Gene Harrington, who after racing it to some success—including a podium finish at Road America—simply parked the car in storage when the series ended. And there it sat for the next 15 years, untouched.

"The car just deteriorated on all fronts," Nash says. "Critters were living in it, and in order to race it again, the hydraulics, wiring, and fuel cell were in need of replacement."

Bill Abel had heard about Harrington's old racer from his friend Scott Harrington—Gene's son—former Shelby Can Am Champion (1992). The younger Harrington named a price, and Abel bought it.

After so many years, it needed a complete restoration. The once flowing bodywork was in rough shape,

and the restoration was a major job. Able reached out to Larry Nash for the restoration.

Nash returned to his old notes from when he campaigned Shelby Can Ams for various drivers in the mid-1990s. He wanted to source the original contractors—gears were particularly difficult to locate.

Soon, however, a rapid restoration was under way to prep the car for a vintage event in Sebring. The car's completion date was estimated at just 60 days. New plumbing, electrics, bodywork, paint, and a complete mechanical overhaul was completed, and the car was once again ready to hit the track.

Today, the car is perhaps the best, most complete Shelby Can Am on the planet. And it is again being driven in anger on vintage road racing circuits. "I didn't restore it to sit in a museum," Abel says. "I wanted to race it again."

CHAPTER 24
One Lewd Limo

by Mark Henderson

During the 1960s, leading NASCAR teams had little trouble finding factory sponsors with plenty of cash and engineering support. Factory-based crews enjoyed huge advantages in horsepower, handling, and aerodynamics. Ford, MOPAR, and Chevy brands typically dominated, so it was less common when other marques placed significantly well during races. It was an especially tough time for independent racers overall.

Roy Tyner stood out as one of the independents to contend with. He was a Native American, which helped earn him nicknames like "The Flying Indian" and "The Wild Indian." He was a self-educated race driver known around the track for his perpetual half-grin, although peers often maintained their distance due to his generous temper, which he was known to flash as well. Tyner frequently drove Fords and Dodges but was most renowned for his ostentatious red, white, and blue 1969 Pontiac Grand Prix stock

The one-time red, white, and blue Pepsi NASCAR Grand National Pontiac of Roy Tyner somehow became gold and it eventually sat forgotten in a Delaware junkyard.

Restored to its historic livery, Tyner's behemoth Grand Prix is in sharp contrast to the much smaller, "jelly bean"–appearing Cup cars for today. The car was restored and is owned today by Pontiac historian Dr. Keith Vrabec of Pennsylvania.

car. Friends regularly quipped, "Roy, what are you doing with a car that looks like *that*?"

The Pepsi-sponsored car ran the circuit in 1969 and 1970, including the first Talladega race. Its heartbeat came from a factory Ram Air V engine and its specifically tuned Pontiac-based chassis. Strangely, the car included a tilt steering wheel and power windows in the rear, so colleagues often dubbed it "Roy's Limousine." Adding to its notoriety, the Grand Prix was the cover feature in the August 1969 issue of *Stock Car Racing* magazine.

Eventually Tyner retired from racing, opened his own auto body business, and occasionally worked as a show car driver for Junior Johnson. His death in 1989 was somewhat suspicious, and the case remains a mystery to this day.

Tyner's Grand Prix somehow wound up in a Delaware junkyard, and its later history is uncertain. The Pepsi team colors were replaced with a blue-over-gold palette, and the number was changed. The engine and transmission were missing. The vehicle had obviously seen its share of abuse and neglect—the chassis and body panels were in terrible shape.

Eventually, the forgotten stock car was rediscovered by Dr. Keith Vrabec, of Wilkes-Barre, Pennsylvania. Dr. Vrabec is an avid admirer of 1969–1972 Pontiac Grand Prix models and a notable collector. In late 1991, an ad in *Hemmings Motor News* caught his attention. With some effort and negotiation, a deal was made, and Vrabec retrieved the car. Its restoration, though, would have to wait a while.

Finally, in 2009, Vrabec contracted the restoration to Vintage Mechanical Works in Sterling, Illinois. A Ram Air IV 400 cubic-inch motor was built to replace the missing engine. A Dearborn three-speed transmission coupled power to a Ford 9-inch rear end, featuring 3.50:1 gears. The race-specific chassis, steering, and suspension were fully refurbished. The restored stock car received high praise when it debuted at Darlington Raceway in September, 2010. Three of Tyner's old team members were even there and shed tears of joy as they were reunited with the car.

Surely, somewhere, Tyner's half-grin has now grown into a permanent smile.

CHAPTER 25
Backroom Beauty

After World War II, many soldiers returned home to their hot rod hobby with newfound skills, thanks to Uncle Sam. Dick Troutman and Tom Barnes were two such ex-GIs.

After the war, Troutman and Barnes worked in the machine and airplane industry before working on Indy cars for Frank Kurtis. Eventually they went into business for themselves and founded Troutman Barnes, a fabrication business.

Troutman Barnes was responsible for many road racing cars of the 1950s, including Jim Hall's Chaparral 1 and Lance Reventhlow's all-conquering Scarabs. Besides customer cars, the team occasionally built racers of their own, including the first Troutman Barnes Special, which was raced by Chuck Daigh in the 1950s. But we're not going to talk about that car.

We're going to talk about the Troutman Barnes Special II, a rear engine car that was built in 1964.

"Racer Buck Fulp called Troutman Barnes and asked them to build him a Special to go racing," Jim Gallucci, the car's owner since 1998, says. "They installed a Chevy engine and Fulp raced it in 1964. But the tube chassis was not in style anymore, so after the season Buck parked it and bought a new Lola T-70 to race Can Am in 1965."

Gallucci is no stranger to this era of racing; he's owned as many as five vintage Can Am racers at any given time. But the 1964 Troutman Barnes Special II was built and raced just prior to the Can Am.

Outdated, the Special II was returned to Troutman Barnes, where it was stored until the late 1960s. "The car was basically worthless at that time," Gallucci says.

The car was eventually sold to master aluminum fabricator Jack Hagemann, who stored it for the next 35 to 40 years. Gallucci occasionally visited Hagemann to talk racing, and he had always dreamed of purchasing all of Hagemann's shop equipment, but never mentioned it to him. One day, though, he noticed all the equipment from his shop was gone.

Back in the day, Chuck Daigh drove this pre–Can Am era Troutman and Barnes Special on West Coast circuits. When its tube-frame was deemed outdated, the car was relegated into the back room of a machine shop. JIM GALLUCCI COLLECTION

Gallucci discovered and purchased the historic car and, after a thorough restoration, today races it in vintage racing events.
JIM GALLUCCI COLLECTION

"Jack (Hagemann) was 95 years old and had sold everything because he didn't know I was interested," Gallucci says. But Hagemann hadn't totally liquidated his shop. "Knowing I was disappointed, Jack said, 'I've still got something for you.' In the back room, under all sorts of shit, was Buck Fulp's old racecar, complete down to the original Halibrand kidney bean wheels. I bought it on the spot."

When Gallucci called Fulp to inform him of his recent purchase, Fulp relayed a great story. "He told me that when he drove back from California to South Carolina with his new racecar on a trailer," Gallucci says, "he pulled into a hotel one night only to find the trailer missing. Buck called the police, and it took a couple of days for them to find the racecar and trailer sitting on a field off the highway."

These days, Gallucci races the Special II in West Coast vintage sports car races. "It's not the fastest car; these cars don't need to be fast," he says. "But she drives like a sweetheart."

CHAPTER 26
One Sexy Southern Sabel

Car sleuth Chuck Goldsborough has the good luck of stumbling across terrific cars that have been long forgotten. For example, in a dusty barn in Australia, he discovered a 1928 Triumph Model W with *zero miles* on it—read more about it in chapter 3, *Vincent in the Barn*.

That's just one, though—he's found scores of terrific sports and racing cars, usually closer to his home in Baltimore, Maryland. This story recounts the tale of a Porsche sports racer, which was originally built in his fair city, even though he didn't discover it near Baltimore.

To most collectors, Goldsborough's car appears to be a Devin, a fiberglass-bodied sports car built by Bill Devin in the 1950s and 1960s. Goldsborough's similarly styled car is a Sabel, however, the first of just 38 Sabels built by John Sabel in Baltimore.

Goldsborough's Sabel had been raced in the 1960s, powered initially by a Porsche 356 engine. It was later converted to a 140-horsepower Corvair engine. It raced at Watkins Glen, VIR, Upper Marlboro, Cumberland, and Summit Point raceways. It also participated in hill climbs at Hershey, Duryea, and Mount Washington. The highlight in the car's career was when it finished second in D Sports Racer in the 1967 SCCA Runoffs at Daytona.

"A friend of mine told me it was on eBay, but I missed it," Goldsborough says. "But eventually I was able to purchase the car off the guy who bought it off eBay. It was hidden away in a barn in Florida for 30 years, from about 1970 until 2000."

The car is now being restored for vintage racing with the original 356 engine and Porsche gauges. And according to Goldsborough, John Sabel is even assisting in the car's restoration. It's rare to find a car like this and have the time and ability to restore it—it's even rarer still to restore it with the original builder in the shop.

Back in the day, 1967, Chuck Goldsborough's Sabel sports racer finished second in the D Sports Racer category at the Daytona SCCA Runoffs. CHUCK GOLDSBOROUGH COLLECTION

CHAPTER 27
Two For The Price Of One

East Coast vintage racer E. B. Odom needed an MGB parts car so he could properly restore his MGB racecar. He located a worthy candidate in Alabama, but the car's owner said, "You can have the MGB only if you clean out the rest of the barn." The owner had recently sold his farm and was being pressured by the real estate agent to vacate the "junk" from the barn.

Besides the MGB, that junk included a 1957 Elva MK II sports racer. And that's where fellow vintage racer Paul Wilson enters the story. Wilson is never one to shy away from interesting sports and racecar restoration projects. He learned about the Elva after it had been moved to Tim Handy's race shop in Virginia.

"It had been crashed, then disassembled," says the retired English professor from Fairfield, Virginia.

When he got the Elva home and was sorting through the parts, this is what it looked like. The Elva was part of an MGB package deal: "If you want the MGB, you must take the Elva!" PAUL WILSON

What started out as a pile of junk became a competitive and beautiful vintage racecar. The car is one of just a few with mostly original drivetrain and suspension components.
PAUL WILSON

"Thankfully the engine was complete and assembled, because the last Coventry Climax engine I bought was totally apart and stored in old boxes. I had to pick up parts with a shovel. It was so bad, I picked through the dirt and found an engine main bearing cap."

Thankfully, that was not the case with this engine.

Elva Cars was a UK-based racecar manufacturer founded in 1955 by Frank Nichols. Nichols noticed that fellow cottage manufacturer Colin Chapman was selling so many Lotus 11s to American racers that he decided to follow Chapman's lead. Elva's first US importer was Continental Motors, in Washington. Elva produced sports racers, sports cars, and formula racecars until 1968.

Wilson believes his Elva—#100-35—was the second MK II built of a production run of probably 12 to 15. "This car was likely driven by racer Frank Baptista at the 1957 Nassau Speed Weeks," Wilson says. "And it was track-tested by Charlie Kolb for a *Sports Car Illustrated* story. This car won the

Mid-West SCCA Regional Championship in 1961 or 1962, driven by Frank Opalka."

Like the Lotus 11, Wilson's Elva is powered by an 1100 cc Coventry Climax engine. Despite the car's sloppy disassembly and storage in the Alabama barn, Wilson says his car was remarkably complete. "It still has the original frame, body, De Dion rear suspension, engine, gearbox, brakes, and suspension, which is so rare for an old racecar."

Wilson completed the Elva's restoration in 2002. He restored all the car's aluminum bodywork, fabrication, paint, and engine himself. Since then, he has raced the car on Southwestern road circuits a couple of times each season.

"The car is a very friendly car to race," he says. "It has light understeer and is very forgiving. But the brakes do tend to fade. Back in the day, these Elvas won their fair share of races, even against those hormone-induced Lotus 11s."

CHAPTER 28
They Call It The Motown Missile

For a young Eara Merritt, one *Hot Rod* magazine image stands out more than any other: that of the Pro Stock driver Don Carleton launching the Motown Missile from the starting line at the 1972 Pomona Nationals, wheels reaching for the sky. It was an iconic image that stayed with Merritt throughout his adult life.

But his automotive interests didn't favor Chrysler products. Merritt liked Fords, especially Shelby products. "I used to go to all the Shelby conventions in the early days," says the 66-year-old civil and mechanical engineer. "That's where I met Mark Williamson and his brother Dan, two straggly guys from Canada who used to hang around with me at those Shelby meets."

Like Merritt, Mark Williamson fell in love with Shelby Mustangs, but never seemed to have enough money to purchase one. "I'd see Mark at Shelby meets year after year, and we became friends," Merritt says. "One day in 1983 or '84, he called and said he found an old racecar that quite possibly could have been the original Motown Missile. It was for sale for $5,000, and he wanted my advice on the car's value. I told him to buy it, then we lost track of each other for the next 20 years."

In 2007, though, Williamson called Merritt and asked if he'd like to ride to Amelia Island Concours d'Elegance with him. "Of course!" Merritt said.

En route to Florida, Merritt asked, "What ever happened to that old Cuda drag car you bought?"

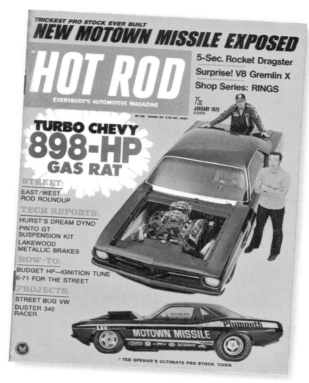

By being nice to a couple of Canadian vintage car enthusiasts, Merritt was able to negotiate a transfer of ownership for a wheel-standing factory 'Cuda. Merritt had the car brought from Ottawa to a restoration shop near Jackson, Mississippi.
EARA MERRITT

"Oh," Williamson said, "it's sitting in my backyard."

Merritt almost had a stroke. The image of the wheel-standing Motown Missile from *Hot Rod* magazine from 40 years earlier came to mind. Williamson showed him a photograph of the decrepit racecar, which had sat beside his house for the past 20 years.

One of the most prolific Super Stock racecars in history, the former Motown Missile was featured in many magazines in the 1970s. After a terrific racing career, the 1971 'Cuda was put out to pasture. EARA MERRITT COLLECTION

It was too much. "How about selling it to me?" Merritt asked.

"I'll think about it," Williamson said.

One year went by, then two. Finally, in 2010, Merritt made Williamson an offer: "Mark, I'll pay for the restoration, and we'll be partners in the car." Williamson agreed.

The car was moved from Ottawa to Star, Mississippi, and into Paul's Body Shop, Merritt's favorite restoration garage. And there it sat for two years as they researched, documented, and collected the right parts to complete the restoration. Merritt even had the car's original car builder, Dick Oldfield, verify that the car was the authentic Motown Missile.

In 2012, the car went into "full restoration mode," according to Merritt. It was dipped in acid for the

second time in its life; when it was new, it had been dipped first to make it lighter for drag racing, and now it was dipped again to remove decades of rust and corrosion.

The restoration took a sabbatical for a little while in 2012, when it was brought to the annual East Coast Drag Racing Hall of Fame in Henderson, North Carolina. There it was united with the three other Motown Missiles that were built and raced from 1970 to 1972.

"It was just out of the dip-tank, and it looked like the photos of the car when it was first built in 1971," Merritt says. "This was a bonafide Chrysler factory racecar that was built to make the Hemi the dominant engine in drag racing."

The rest, as they say, is history.

CHAPTER 29
New Body For An Old Girl

by Mark Henderson

True American sports cars were rare in the early 1950s. Just about the only way to *own* one was to *build* one. Lean, muscular bodywork was sought, but few choices were available. Two men made it their goal to help the custom American sports car lover. In 1951 or 1952, William "Doc" Boyce-Smith and Hugh Jorgenson collaborated to form the Victress Manufacturing Company. Their goal was to produce sports car bodies that could "out Jag the Jag." The fiberglass Victress S1A body was their first offering.

Another set of gentlemen—brothers Guy and Joe Mabee, of Midland, Texas—was famous for fast cars and sponsorship of up-and-coming drivers like young

Carroll Shelby. The Mabees wanted an American racecar that could compete both on the track and the salt flats, so they hired Denny Larson to create one. The project began by mating a 1952 S1A body to a custom chrome-moly chassis. Ray Brown built a 331 cubic-inch Chrysler Hemi with a Chet Herbert cam, Hilborn injection, and a Harmon-Collins magneto. Power was delivered through a top-loader three-speed into a Halibrand rear end. The "Mabee Special" was driven to a record 203.105 mph at Bonneville in 1953. Over time, it was an SAC/SCCA road racing contender, competitive in the quarter-mile drags and even at Pikes Peak.

The Mabees sold the Victress in 1955, and it was

Joe Mabee drove the Mabee Special to a 203.105 mph record at Bonneville in 1953.
THE ROBINSON COLLECTION

When Bruce Gross rediscovered the car in 1983, a one-off aluminum body had replaced the ruined original S1A unit. THE ROBINSON COLLECTION

the first of many new owners for the Special. It was totaled during a 1960 road race on the Ascarate course in El Paso. The original S1A shell was destroyed, so that particular owner had the car rebuilt with a one-off aluminum body and then continued to race it in competition. Then the car disappeared in 1965.

Almost 20 years later, in 1983, Bruce Gross found the car's remains on a ranch in Mexico. He wasn't exactly sure what it was, but he knew it was unique and needed to be rescued. It took Bruce 10 years to convince the current owner to sell, but eventually he was successful. He trailered it over the border and stored it behind his business in El Paso.

In 1998, Jim and Lea Ann Robinson were vacationing in southern Texas. They noticed the car

behind a commercial building and were able to learn a bit about its colorful history. With their interest piqued, they were pleasantly surprised to be able to negotiate its purchase.

Now it was time to restore the Mabee Special. The five-year restoration began by locating a donor car with a restorable S1A body. The Robinsons befriended a man named Denny Larson, who helped verify their car's authenticity. They met with Ray Brown and found another 1952 Hemi to rebuild the Special to its proper specifications. The car needed a transmission, and a Chevy T-10 was selected. The Halibrand rear end was converted to 4.10 gears to improve drivability. The four corners were outfitted with 6.50x16-inch Firestones installed on Halibrand knock-offs. Jim Robinson completed the bodywork and paint, and Ed Dickson recreated the lettering.

The restored Mabee Special has attended multiple Concours d'Elegance events nationwide and was displayed at Bonneville for the 50th anniversary of its speed record. The Robinsons are quick to acknowledge all those who played a role in its heritage. In particular, they hope that Guy and Joe Mabee are proud of the car's continuing legacy.

CHAPTER 30

Quarter-Mile Cobra

When Carroll Shelby conceived the Cobra in 1962, it was with road racing in mind. He envisioned a dominant vehicle for endurance events at tracks like Sebring, Le Mans, and Daytona. When drag racers saw the small car with the powerful engine, though, they thought about shorter events—just one-quarter mile, even.

Shelby American actually built six Cobras specifically for drag racing. They were known as Dragonsnakes, but many more were assembled by independent Cobra owners around the country.

Our story concerns chassis number CSX 2353—one of those independent drag racers.

When the car left the Shelby factory in California, it was a standard 289 Cobra equipped with a hardtop, chrome wire wheels, large oil pan, and even a luggage rack. At some point, it was converted to full drag specs, including huge rear wheels, tiny magnesium front wheels, headers, rollbar, Weber carburetors, wheelie bars, and no front brakes—and lettered in gold-leaf: *Sieben & Skinner, a West Coast team.*

Not much is known about the car's history until it came into the possession of race driver Salt Walther.

The early racing history of independent Comp Cobra #CSX 2353 is a little bit sketchy. The car was apparently drag raced on the West Coast before landing in race driver Salt Walther's Ohio sports car dealership in the 1970s. JIM MAXWELL

The car features a full roll cage, magnesium wheels, and no front brakes. The car was wrecked during a late-night demonstration ride and has sat in this body shop for 40-plus years. JIM MAXWELL

In the 1970s, Walther advertised the car for sale in his specialty dealership for $5,000, but the story is that Walther's brother took a young lady for a joy ride in the car one night. At high speed, the brakes failed, and Walther's brother crashed the car into a lake.

The car was sold by Walther—complete with bent sheetmetal—to the owner of a body shop and towing business. "I don't remember what I paid for it," he says.

The damaged car was parked in a garage in the 1970s, where it still remains today. Who knows what lies in store for this racer from another era?

CHAPTER 31

Doc's Time Capsule Cycles

like many who today make their livings on the business side of professional motorsports, Mark Coughlin began his career as an amateur racer himself. He raced motorcycles on Northeast road courses in Bridgehampton (NY), Loudon (NH), and Pocono (PA).

In his 20s, Coughlin admits he was a decent amateur in the 350 cc class. But walking through the paddocks of these tracks on race weekends, he always admired the professional teams with trick factory racing bikes and the talented technicians hunched over them.

Realizing that lack of funding—and possibly talent—would prevent him from ever achieving a chance to race a factory Honda, Kawasaki, or Yamaha, he decided to pursue opportunities in motorsports elsewhere.

Coughlin's career in motorsports is significant. He's managed Valvoline's North American racing activities, as well as spent time with both Ford and

Coughlin is now the proud owner of not one but three of "Doc" Kieffer's old cycles.

Dr. Dave "Doc" Kieffer raced motorcycles for almost 30 years, and was an inspiration to Mark Coughlin.

Jaguar. Today, at 55 years old, Coughlin is executive vice president of Consulting for Octagon Sports Marketing. It's a lofty position, one where he occasionally enjoys conversations with Formula One Chief Bernie Ecclestone, NASCAR CEO Brian France, and drivers from every area of professional motorsport.

But deep down inside, Coughlin is a racer, and motorcycle racing is what he still craves.

As a young racer, one of the riders he admired from a distance was semi-pro Dr. Dave "Doc" Kieffer, a renowned orthopedic surgeon from Wyoming who road-raced motorcycles for almost 30 years.

"Doc pieced together lots of the pro riders when they got hurt in racing accidents," Coughlin says, "so they gave him all the super-trick factory race parts for his bikes when they were a season old. Doc bought Ducati, Honda, and Kawasaki street bikes for, say, $7,000, then bought the $25,000 race kits to make them track-ready."

Rare factory front forks and engine pieces often wound up in his transporter on race weekends. They were gifts from his rider friends. According to Coughlin, Kieffer bought and raced dozens of bikes. When he was done racing the bikes, he stored them in his workshop in Laramie, Wyoming.

"He did it right," Coughlin says. "He had a new box truck to haul his equipment, and he flew his own airplane to the track."

Kieffer raced for probably 30 years, and decided to hang up his leathers in the mid-'90s. In Laramie, the bikes sat silent for nearly 20 years before Coughlin heard a rumor in 2012 that Kieffer might consider selling his race bike collection.

Coughlin flew from North Carolina to Colorado. Then he drove to Wyoming. There, he says, he walked into a "motorcycle racing time capsule."

Kieffer gave Coughlin the opportunity to have first option on his collection of bikes. He purchased three significant bikes: a 1982 Kawasaki Moriwaki 1000 cc AMA Formula One bike, a 1986 Honda VF750 RK Superbike, and a 1988 Honda RC30, plus crates of brand new, extremely rare factory "Team Only" parts.

All three bikes have significant factory and pro racing history. "I've hired a pro rider to race these bikes at vintage races," Coughlin says. "I feel fortunate to be able to finally live an era that I could only admire from a distance as a kid. I didn't have a pot to piss in when I club raced, but today, I like the team owner role."

CHAPTER 32

The Golden Dragster

In 1975, drag racers Don Nicholson and Bob Glidden raced sister 1970 Mustangs.

"Back then, running a long wheelbase car with a small-block engine gave you an advantage over a Mustang II or a Pinto," says professional barnfinder Lars Ekberg. "You could back-date the body five years, which is why they built a '70 Mustang."

After Nicholson raced this Mustang for a season or two, it changed hands and engines often. Over the next few years, the Mustang had been powered by everything from a Ford 427 SOHC to a Chrysler Hemi. Ekberg's friend Keith Bronson bought the car in the late 1970s and raced it with a 428 Cobra Jet engine borrowed from his brother's Drag Pac Torino.

"I met Keith in the mid-1980s when I bought the Cobra Jet engine out of the car," he says. "At that time, he told me the car was a sister to Bob Glidden's car. He

Lars Ekberg purchased an old drag car from his friend who told him it was a sister car to Bob Gliddon's Mustang. Well, it was actually Don Nicholson's Prostock Mustang! TOM COTTER

Ekberg's plan is to restore the car to the gold and yellow paint scheme that Nicholson raced it in 1975.
TOM COTTER

installed a 460 engine and a 1969 front end because the 1970 sheetmetal was no longer available."

Ekberg wound up purchasing the Mustang from Bronson in 2007. When he picked up the car, Bronson again repeated that it was a sister car to Glidden's and that it was constructed by Don Hardy, a top Pro Stock chassis builder in Texas. "I called Don at his Texas shop, explained the car to him, and emailed photos to him the next day," Ekberg says.

"Yup, it's one of mine," Hardy confirmed.

Ekberg used a DA sander and took off at least six layers of paint until he got down to the original gold and yellow paint scheme that Nicholson ran in 1975. "The rumors were that this car was wrecked and that it had been converted to a Pinto or a Fairmont," he says.

Pro Stock rules at the time required that the cars resemble their street counterparts, so the car had airbrushed gauges and a clock on the dashboard, which remain to this day. But Ekberg hadn't realized the

"liberties" Hardy had taken when constructing the car originally.

"The NHRA didn't use templates, so a stock Mustang windshield doesn't come close to fitting," Ekberg says. "It's basically two-thirds of a true Mustang in size. The roof is lowered, the quarter-panels are sucked in, and the windshield pillars are slanted back."

Ekberg's plans are to restore the car back to its 1975 specs. So far, he's purchased a set of high-port heads and a tunnel-port intake manifold while walking through the All-Ford Show in Columbus. "And I found a 1975 XE Cleveland block that was raced at 366 cubic inches," he says. "It'll probably turn 750 to 800 horsepower at 10,000 rpm. I'll probably make a few passes with the car when it's done at an historic race, but I don't want to stuff it into a wall. I first saw this car race in Pennsylvania when I was fifteen years old."

VI

RARER THAN HEN'S TEETH

CHAPTER 33
Fast, Hot, And Rare

Jeff Trask and his wife were driving in California's Central Valley, looking for real estate for a second home. "We were about six hours from our home in Santa Ana, and looking in the Mariposa and Grass Valley areas," Trask says.

Until recently, Trask had owned a yacht dealership in Newport Beach before selling it and becoming a full-time car hunter. "We were driving with a realtor through the area of Murphys, Angels Camp, and Sutter Creek," he says, "all old mining towns. We had

already spent a couple of days with the realtor when he mentioned, 'Your wife tells me you're into old Porsches.'"

Trask said yes, he was, and the realtor continued: "Well, I have one of those."

Trask's brain switched gears from house-mode to Porsche-mode. "What do you have?" he asked.

"It's an old convertible that's been parked since 1979," the realtor said. "I haven't driven it since. It's at my farm—would you like to see it?"

Not wanting to appear too excited, Trask casually

The longtime owner of this Porsche Speedster bought it in 1962 and parked it under this lean-to in 1979. He casually mentioned to Jeff Trask that he owned an old Porsche, and Trask bought it in 2007.
JEFF TRASK

mentioned that he'd be interested in seeing the car before they left for home the next day. Plans were made to meet the next morning.

"My wife wasn't too into it because we had a long drive ahead of us," he says, "but we met the realtor on a street corner in the small town of Galt the next day."

The realtor's overgrown driveway was only a mile from Galt's downtown. "We drove through two-foot tall grass, and when we got to the end, I could see a Porsche-shaped vehicle in a car port under a tarp," Trask says.

When the tarp was peeled away, Trask saw one of the most desirable Porsches ever built: a 1958 Speedster. Sheltered under the carport, the car appeared to be sound and dry.

Trask whipped out his Porsche 356 reference book, which he never leaves home without. "The numbers totally matched," he says. "It was an untouched, original car."

The realtor told his story of owning the Porsche. He grew up and went to college in Oregon. In 1962,

he bought the Speedster from the original owner and used it as his daily driver until moving to California to pursue a career in real estate.

"He realized it wouldn't be very practical to haul clients around in, so he parked it in the carport in 1979, where it sat for almost 30 years," he says. The R\ realtor told Trask he might be interested in selling it, but only after he spoke with his son.

A few days went by, and Trask wondered if he was going to ever hear back from the realtor. Then the phone rang. "He had spoken to his son, who was not interested in the Porsche," Trask says. So he made an offer and it was accepted.

"In the world of hunting Porsche 356s, the two Holy Grails are the Speedster and the 550 Spider. I found one: now I'm looking for the other."

Hopefully another house won't be an expensive addendum to the Spider.

CHAPTER 34
The Professor's Rotten Secret

The car was described as being so deteriorated that it appeared as if it were parked next to a lawn sprinkler for 30 years.

A shame, for sure, because the car is extremely rare. Only 442 were built.

The car, a 1964 Porsche 356 C 2000GS, is the last of the original Carrera series. It had been purchased by American Dr. Eric Haron—an Oxford professor and Porsche enthusiast living in England—from a German dealer in 1967.

Heron once brought the Porsche with him to the United States when he attended Harvard during a sabbatical. When he returned to England with the Porsche, he had the red car repainted black, then put it into long-term storage in a carport with a lattice roof. In other words, the car sat for 30 years virtually exposed to the elements.

British architect John Heah purchased the Porsche in 2007, but again it sat until 2011, when it was given a rapid, eight-month restoration. Then the car was sent to 356 specialist John Willhoit in Long Beach, California, who "replaced all the sheetmetal from the doorhandles down," says Peter Linsky, who wrote about the car for *Excellence* magazine.

The 2-liter four-cam engine was restored by Bill Doyle in Jackson, Wyoming. The better-than-new restoration was introduced at the 2011 Concours on the Avenue in Carmel, California, where Linsky first saw the car.

"It was a knockout," he says, "just stunning."

The Porsche has also been displayed at the Dana Point Concours and The Quail at Monterey. The car will be shown at the Amelia Island Concours before returning to England, where it may enjoy slightly better storage conditions this time around.

British Porsche racing legend Eric Struder restored this Carrera after it was exhumed from its prison cell after so many years. The car was rotted up to its door handles. Stored for many decades inside this stall, this rare Porsche, which has a porous roof, was exposed to the wet and humid British weather for 30-plus years. JOHN HEAH

CHAPTER 35

Trailer Treasure

We've all heard the rumors—someone on the other side of town has a rare collector vehicle: a one-off muscle car, a Duesenberg, a Le Mans-winning Ferrari. . . . Most of the time, these are either fictional or a misunderstood whisper, like when an amateur turns a Fiat into a Ferrari.

Skip Lecates, of York, Pennsylvania, has heard all the stories, but one tale about a Yenko Nova kept circulating among area enthusiasts. "I started hearing that rumor about fifteen years ago; that it was in the nearby town of Red Lion," he says. "I started a real push to find the car."

One Saturday in May 2012, Lecates left his home determined not to return until he found the car. He kept snooping and eventually came to a long, wooded driveway. He turned into it, not knowing where he'd end up. But he finally found a pair of trailers, there among the forest.

Bingo. He had heard the car was stored in a trailer. "I didn't know if I'd be shot," he says, remembering his walk toward the house.

The owner of the Yenko Deuce had bought it for his wife in 1970. It had a 360-horsepower LT1 engine with solid lifters and an automatic shift on the column. Yenko added SS Wheels, striping, swaybars, mirrors, and a hood tach. It retailed for about $5,000.

The car had been in the trailer since about 1987.

The owner named a price, Lecates liked it, and by Wednesday of the next week the car was his. He trailered it home a few days after. "A friend of mine got all worked up about it, so I sold it to him the following Monday," Lecates says.

For Lecates, it was easy come, easy go. "Right now I am persistent on finding a 1970 L78 Nova," he says. A barn-finder's work is never done!

The Yenko Deuce sees the light of day for the first time in decades. CHICK RENN

The Yenko Deuce had an automatic, a 360 HP LT1 engine and 123,000 miles on the odometer. CHICK RENN

CHAPTER 36
Follow Mr. Finger

Because I've written several barn-find books, I'm often asked to talk to groups about finding old cars. I usually discuss the same theme: talk to everyone you know about old cars; look behind houses and garages; and make friends with deliverymen, policemen, and landscapers, people who can legally enter private property.

I was asked to speak at the Carolina's Region of the Sports Car Club of America at their annual awards banquet in Spartanburg, South Carolina. I gave my dog-and-pony show after dinner, answered a few questions, and went back to my seat.

When I got there, my friend and tablemate John Finger asked me, "What would be your ultimate barn-find?"

"Well," I said to John, "it had always been a Cobra, but I found one of those. So my next ultimate barn-find would be a Cunningham. But that would be insane, because there are only twenty-five in the world."

Constructor Briggs Cunningham wanted to win the 24 Hours of Le Mans in an American car with American drivers. But the organizers wouldn't allow him to enter a car unless he was an automobile manufacturer, similar to Ferrari, Aston Martin, and Jaguar. So he reluctantly became a manufacturer of 20 coupes and 5 convertibles.

John pondered my choice for a moment. Then, he leaned in and whispered, "I know where a Cunningham is. A friend of mine owns it. It's in Greenville, the next town over."

For me, finding a Cunningham was like finding the Hope Diamond. I found this one in a Greenville, South Carolina, basement. It is the second C-3 built, and had spent 56 years in Greenville among four different owners. MARK COUGHLIN

I started sweating. *Oh, my God,* I thought. *Can this be real?*

Then the cynical part of my conscience took over. I thought that there is no way a real barn-find Cunningham could exist; with 25 in the world, they are all certainly owned by millionaire car collectors. It must be a mistake. It must be some kind of fiberglass kit car, probably with a Corvair engine.

Then John said, "I'll bring you there next week."

That week couldn't come fast enough. On the prescribed day, I met John in front of a generic metal storage building in Greenville. We walked into the

This is the same car when it was new. It is shown on display at the 1952 Concours D'Elegance, held in conjunction with that year's Grand Prix. Finding the car was terrific; finding color photos is icing on the cake.
BILL GILTZOW COLLECTION

building, and son-of-a-bitch, there sat a genuine C-3 Cunningham, ridden hard and put away wet.

I told the owner, Sam Henderson, "I need to buy that car." Sam told me it wasn't for sale, but that if he ever did decide to sell it, I would have first option.

It took several years of staying in touch with Sam, but one day he called and said he was ready to sell. With a trailer in tow, I drove from my home in Davidson, North Carolina, to Sam's place in Greenville.

Which car was it? Were there any serial numbers? More importantly, could I even afford it?

Well, there was no serial number, but there was an engine number, and I could barely afford it. It wasn't

cheap, but acquiring dreams seldom are. But I knew I was the owner of one rare Cunningham.

It was #5207, the second Cunningham C-3 coupe built. It was built in West Palm Beach, Florida, and the body was installed at Vignale in Turin, Italy. It had a 331 cubic-inch Chrysler Hemi engine, and a three-speed Cadillac gearbox. Cunningham #5207 was used as the media car, the car used by journalists for magazine stories and road tests.

Dreams seldom come true, but lucky for me, I scored a real gem.

CHAPTER 37
The Old Cobra

The *World Registry of Cobras* lists chassis number CSX 2511, the 511th Cobra built, with a black body and interior, and delivered from Shelby American to Jack Meffert Ford in Springfield, Ohio. It was equipped with chrome wire wheels, a hard top, and two four-barrel carburetors.

During a test drive, CSX 2511 was involved in a serious accident, and the vehicle was totaled. With just 45 miles on the odometer, it was sold as scrap to the owner of a towing business, who purchased it as a parts car for his drag-racing Cobra. The wreck was parked in a lot, where it sat for 45 years. Little-by-little, the towing company operator dismantled the crashed Cobra, and stored the pieces in an old box truck body.

He intended to eventually rebuild the wreck, though, and ordered new front fenders and rear quarter panels from Shelby. He hung the new fenders on the garage wall, where they still hang today, nearly 50 years later.

Eventually, as the car became more valuable, it was moved into a storage unit, but not before significant deterioration had occurred. The top and tool kit in the trunk, which should have been perfect, had deteriorated to dust.

"When we decided to move the car inside, I had to cut a tree down that had grown up through the engine compartment," says Mitch, son of the towing company operator.

Today, the car sits as a sad time capsule—a totally doused, demolished Cobra, with only 45 miles on the odometer.

This Cobra, CSX 2511, was wrecked during a dealership test drive. One of the occupants was killed and the car was junked with just 45 miles on the odometer. JIM MAXWELL

Much of the last 45 years, CSX 2511 sat outside, deteriorating badly. The owners finally parked the car inside a truck body. JIM MAXWELL

CHAPTER 38
Built For Speed

Original AC Cobras are considered rare because only 998 were built. Ferrari GTOs are even rarer because just 33 were built. Rarer yet is the Cunningham C-3, because only 20 coupes and 5 convertibles were built in the early 1950s.

Imagine, then, how rare Roger Morrison's 1952 Sorrell SR-100 is, with probably just six built.

The difference, of course, is that Shelby American, B.S. Cunningham, and Ferrari were factories (albeit small factories). Sorrell's were constructed in his Englewood, California, shop, which was little more than an oversized garage.

Bob Sorrell's creation is called an "American Special," traditionally a purpose-built car using readily available parts, usually from American cars. They were conceived to compete with their more expensive brethren on racetracks, the show circuit, and local drive-ins.

Built in 1953, Morrison's is one of two complete cars known of six roadsters and one coupe built by Sorrell, a fabrication wizard who built streamliner and dragster bodies for racers such as TV Tommy Ivo.

Morrison's Sorrell is presently equipped with a small-block Chevy, but was originally built with a small, early Chrysler Hemi. If he decides to restore the car, a Hemi will again occupy the engine bay.

American Specials were often rather basic in the suspension and mechanical departments, but the car's sleek look disguised its hidden, humble roots. And the lightweight car with American power gave a highly competitive performance. The coupe ran 174 mph at Bonneville in 1955.

"I like the way the front fenders extend to the rear, similar to streamliners," Morrison says. "And the way the passenger compartment is nestled between the two of them."

Probably only six Sorrells were built, making a Sorrell more rare than a Cobra or a Ferrari GTO or a Cunningham. Roger Morrison's discovery is powered by a Chevy small block, but he will restore it with the original engine: a Chrysler Hemi.
ROGER MORRISON

CHAPTER 39
The *Real* Job #1 Mustang

The Mustang coupe sat in a driveway in Winston-Salem, North Carolina, driven hard and put away wet. After passing the car for a few months, Todd Adams knocked on the door and asked if it was for sale.

"No," the woman said. Apparently her father had bought it new and it had sentimental value. But a few more visits convinced her that Adams was a serious buyer.

"I had checked the serial number, #100211, and knew it was a very early Mustang, definitely a Day One car," he says. "That's what purists call it." *Day One* means it was sold on the first day Mustang went on sale, on April 17, 1964.

Adams didn't think much of it, registered it, and drove it to his final year of high school. After he graduated in 1986, he went to college and parked the Mustang in his parent's backyard.

Adams was offered a parking space in a friend's barn in 1992, and there it sat for the next 18 years. Adams almost forgot he even owned the car. "I went 10 years without even speaking to my friend," he says.

Adams was reminded of his vintage Mustang, though, while watching the television broadcast of the 2010 Barrett-Jackson auction. "They showed a 1964 1/2 Mustang Pace Car, and mentioned that it was serial #100212, the oldest production Mustang known to exist," he says. "I said to myself, 'I think my Mustang in the barn is older than that!'"

She ain't pretty, but she sure is rusty! Mustang #100211 is the oldest known production-line Mustang. Owned by Todd Adams of North Carolina, the car was his daily driver when he bought it as a high school senior. STEVE MEZARDJIAN

Hull & Dobbs is the original selling dealership in Winston-Salem, North Carolina. STEVE MEZARDJIAN

#100211 was a real stripper when new: six-cylinder, three speed, 13-inch, four bolt wheels. But it is the earliest production-line Mustang in the world. STEVE MEZARDJIAN

He checked the title, and sure enough, it was #100211. In fact, Adams's car was now the earliest-known Job One Mustang, meaning that it is the oldest-known Mustang to have rolled off the assembly line on the first day of production, on March 9, 1964. Cars built prior to #211 were preproduction, built as prototypes by engineers. When new, his car was loaded onto a transporter and delivered to Hull-Dobbs Ford in Winston-Salem, North Carolina, where it was sold to the father of the woman who sold it to Adams.

After the auction, Adams removed the car from the damp barn and parked it in dry, secure storage where it has remained ever since. And Adams's Mustang is definitely a barn-find—looking sad and in need of restoration, the car even has original crayon markings on the firewall and radiator support.

"The car is a real bastard," he says. "It's a mixture of production and pre-production parts. All the glass is original, and a couple of pieces were 1963 date code production. The only parts on the Mustang that are not original are the front bumper and half of the grille surround."

Adams's life has changed since buying #100211 as a high school senior. He's a successful businessman with a family—and even another vintage Mustang. Realizing that a correct restoration would cost a small fortune, he's inclined to sell it to a collector who would appreciate such a rare car.

CHAPTER 40
One-of-One Abarth

I was walking across the lawn at the 2013 Amelia Island Concours d'Elegance, looking at row upon row of fantastically restored automobiles, when I was stopped in my tracks by a car that was so small, I could almost fit it into my pocket.

It was two-toned—aqua green and white—and it was breathtaking. I had to find out more about this terrific little car.

I met the owner, Elad Shraga, who was quite proud of his barn-find. The car was a 1955 Abarth 208 Spyder, an ideally proportioned two-seat roadster with a decidedly 1950s style.

When its designer, Carlo Abarth, left the Cisitalia car company in 1949, he took with him the muffler division and all the company's racing technology. He started manufacturing Abarth mufflers for European cars, which were required accessories for any dyed-in-the-wool sports car enthusiast in the 1950s and 1960s. No MGA, Alfa Romeo, or Austin Healey would have been complete during that time without the twin chrome-tipped Abarth tailpipes in the back of the car.

But by 1954, he wanted to produce his own car based around the 1,100 cc Fiat engine. He believed that with an aluminum body, the car might be quite competitive. He decided to introduce three cars, probably designed by Giovanni Michelotti: a racing Spyder (convertible); a coupe; and a street Spyder.

The cars were displayed at the 1955 Turin show in Italy. Then they were imported to the United States, but the public had no use for the coupe or the street

Elad Shraga's Abarth Spider is a one of a kind roadster. Built for the 1955 Turin Auto Show, it never excited the public the way the racing version had. So the car was sold to the DuPont family then disappeared for a number of years. ELAD SHRAGA

Spyder—only the racecar mattered. So the threesome was broken up and sold off.

The coupe spent decades in the Midwest and now resides in Holland.

The street Spyder was sold to the DuPont family, who had a sizable collection. They kept the car until the late 1960s. The family gave the car to their airplane mechanic, who crashed it in 1982. He parked the car, and it was not seen again until he connected

After much Internet research, Shraga found the car under a workbench in Queens, New York. The body and mechanicals have been restored, but the original interior has been retained. ELAD SHRAGA

with Shraga in 2006. The owner made a mention on an Abarth website that he owned #005, which got Shraga's attention (but apparently nobody else's).

"It's a family heirloom—I'll never sell," was the owner's response to Shraga's inquiries. Shraga needed to own that car, however, because he already owned the sister racing Spyder, which had shared the show stand with the street Spyder at the 1955 Turin show.

Two years later, the former owner relented, and Shraga was able to purchase the car. When he purchased the vehicle, he was a resident of New York City; now he resides outside Tel Aviv, Israel. When he first contacted the former owner, he was shocked to learn the car had been stored under a workbench in the New York suburb of Queens for decades.

"This Spyder is fascinating," Shraga says. "It's like a time capsule. It still has 1955 tires on it!" After he bought it, a body shop in Connecticut named Draggone Restorations restored the body and mechanics, but Shraga decided to leave the vintage interior alone.

"I am so lucky to own two Abarths that were hidden for 40 years," he says, and "it pays to troll the Internet."

Especially in the barn-find business.

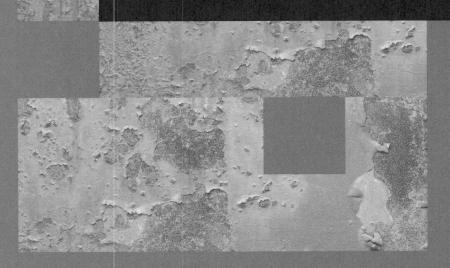

VII

HOLLYWOOD HAS-BEENS

CHAPTER 41
Star-Struck Roller

For some folks, it was *The Honeymooners*. For others, it was *Star Trek* or *Batman*.

For me, it was *Leave It to Beaver*.

For so many of us of the Baby Boomer generation, there seems to be a favorite television show that we remember for decades after the show ceased to be shown. For Jim Inglis, it was *Burke's Law*.

Burke's Law starred Gene Barry as millionaire Amos Burke and featured his faithful chauffer, Henry, and their unusual "squad car," a 1962 Rolls Royce Silver Cloud II. The story revolved around Burke, who even though rich, took the job of being chief of homicide in the LA Police Department. The car played a significant role as it chased down criminals. It even had an on-board telephone, which was quite a novel idea in the 1960s. Inglis never missed an episode, and the theme song stayed in his head into adulthood.

"When I got older and started to collect cars, I sought to find the whereabouts of the Burke Rolls Royce," says the Florida resident. "But California-based Four-Star Productions, who produced the show, was long gone; tracing the license plates proved fruitless; and star Gene Barry was living in a life-care facility."

But Googling *Burke's Law Rolls Royce* put Inglis in touch with a trail of former owners. When the trail ended, the car was in a garage in Vero Beach, Florida, just 60 miles north of Inglis's Palm Beach home.

After a short negotiation, he owned the Rolls.

"After 45 years, my long awaited dream has come true," Inglis says. "It's a 35,000-mile original car, and that's just the way I plan to keep it."

Case closed!

As a kid, Jim Inglis never missed an episode of *Burke's Law*, a TV show about a fictional detective who drove a Rolls Royce. As an adult, many years later, Inglis searched for, discovered, and purchased that very same Rolls! JIM INGLIS

CHAPTER 42
Otherworldly Orbitron

It was hard to escape Ed "Big Daddy" Roth when I was a kid. To young guys in the 1960s, Roth's google-eyed character, Rat Fink, was plastered on T-shirts and his monster cars were all the rage for kids of a certain model-kit-building age.

Roth, an artist, cartoonist, pinstriper, and custom car designer and builder, was all the rage in the '60s, and much of model kit manufacturer Revell's revenues was based on scale versions of Roth's creations. The man was a brand and industry onto himself, having created the weirdo T-shirt craze that others quickly copied. Some of Roth's more memorable automotive creations some readers may remember include Tweedy Pie, Mysterion, Beatnik Bandit, Surfite, Outlaw, and the Road Agent.

As a kid, Beau Boeckmann was also a Roth-freak. Now, Boeckmann has taken his interest to another level—he has established a small museum dedicated to Roth vehicles and memorabilia.

Boeckmann, 43, is vice president of Galpin Motors, a Ford dealership in Los Angeles that his father bought in 1946. So he has literally grown up

After being used as a makeshift dumpster in Mexico, Beau Boeckmann bought the Ed "Big Daddy" Roth Orbitron was purchased and brought it back to California for a full restoration. BEAU BOECKMANN COLLECTION

Purchased by Roth enthusiast Beau Boeckmann, the Orbitron was restored by many of the same contractors who worked on it when the car was new. BEAU BOECKMANN

in the car business. And when the news spread that Roth's Orbitron had been spotted in Mexico after going unseen for decades, Boeckmann was all over it.

It was found by El Paso, Texas–based car hunter Michael Lightbourn. Lightbourn frequently travels south of the border in search of significant American cars that migrated to Mexico and stumbled on Orbitron in the city of Juarez, where it was basically a dumpster in the front of a sex and video shop. The shop's owner was reluctant to sell, but the partly destroyed hot rod had languished in front of that store for years, and Lightbourn convinced the owner to sell.

Orbitron had deteriorated badly over the decades; the unique front nose cone that carried the car's distinguished three-headlight pod was missing, and what remained elsewhere was in poor condition. "Michael [Lightbourn] and I started talking at the 2007 SEMA Show," Boeckmann says. Lightbourn wanted to keep the car and restore it. "But when I told him my vision for the car, we made a deal. So I got on a plane and

flew to El Paso to see the car."

Boeckmann saw the car in all its depressing glory. He and Lightbourn then drove to Juarez to see where the car had been parked for all those years. "I was a little bit nervous, because Juarez is known as the most dangerous city in North America," he says.

Once Boeckmann had the car back in LA, he worked with many of the car's original contractors to assist in the Orbitron's restoration. Larry Watson and Bill Carter painted the car when it was new in 1964; they painted the car again during its restoration. Joe Perez originally stitched the Orbitron's upholstery and was hired by Boeckmann the second time around.

"The toughest part of the restoration was finding the original type TV set that sat in the dashboard," Boeckmann says. "Roth did everything by eye," he adds, "nothing was measured.

"We didn't change any of Roth's techniques during the restoration." So if it's still a little out-of-this-world, well, all the better.

CHAPTER 43

Herbie's Nemesis: The Thorndyke Special

by John Barron

When reader John Barron placed a bid for this rare 1965 Apollo GT on eBay, he had no idea just how special it really was. He discovered the car's past, and submitted the story to an essay contest on www.barnfinds.com. He won the contest, and his prize is having his story appear in this book—congratulations, John!

In February 2004, I saw a 1965 Apollo 5000 GT basket case being offered on eBay. The photos showed a partially primered body, which had suffered from a number of accidents and had significant rust damage as well. The description indicated that the right-side door had been severely damaged and only repaired by an amateur. The car was missing both seats and most of the interior. The engine/trans were strapped in with trailer tie straps, and the rest of the parts were in a bunch of boxes. Just to top it all off, the floors had been cut away and replaced with a poorly designed substitute made of galvanized sheetmetal. All in all, it was a total wreck requiring a total ground-up restoration and some pretty fancy metalwork. That was the bad news.

The good news was that all the necessary parts unique to the car—one of 88 built—were available, albeit in rough shape, and that the seller was willing to deliver the car to anywhere in the continental United States free of charge. In a moment of weakness (madness?), I bid the minimum amount and waited for the auction to play out. Seven days later, I was the proud owner of this very rare basket case, and true to his word, the seller delivered the car from Texas to northern Michigan where I took over and trailered my new beauty home to Toronto, Canada.

So far it was pretty standard stuff (other than the rarity of the car), but it was going to get a lot rarer. While researching the Apollo GT story, I found that a yellow Apollo GT was driven by the villain, Peter Thorndyke, in the 1968 Disney movie *The Love Bug*. The Apollo was known as the Thorndyke Special, and the villain used every dirty trick in the book to

When John Barron purchased his Apollo, it was rough, but it was also seldom seen and interesting. He never realized it had been a Hollywood star at an earlier time in its life. JOHN BARRON

Based on seeing the *Herbie the Lovebug* movie and comparing the collision damage, Barron determined his Apollo was actually the Thorndyke Special. Here it is on display fully restored at Concourso Italiano.
JOHN BARRON

defeat the little VW Bug. The Apollo could dispense oil from the back of the vehicle, there were numerous collisions and near misses, and even a grizzly bear was involved in one scene. This was, of course, all done before the advent of computer-generated graphics.

I finally got a copy of the movie and sat down one night to watch it. About halfway through the movie I began to realize that many of the areas of collision between the VW and the Thorndyke Special corresponded to the damaged areas of my basket case Apollo. Could it be? Subsequent research confirmed that I was, in fact, the owner of the Thorndyke Special, co-star of *The Love Bug*. So much for painting it maroon.

Disney Studios had contracted Max Balchowsky about preparing two Apollo GTs for the movie. He also supplied a number of other cars that were used in various racing scenes. Balchowsky had performed extensive modifications to the engine, suspension, and brakes of the stunt car that was used for the driving/collision scenes. These mods were instrumental in helping identify my car.

Restoration crawled along at the usual snail's pace. The damage to my car after eight on-screen collisions was extensive and required the work of a highly skilled panel beater to rectify. The rest of the restoration required many, many hours of research and hard work to finish the car and to get it right.

Fast forward to August 2013: I was driving the Thorndyke Special across the stage at Concorso Italiano, where I joined 17 other Apollo GTs, which represented 20 percent of the total production for the 50th anniversary of the Apollo. Milt Brown, the creator of the car, was also being honored, as was Ron Plescia, who did the initial design work on the cars, and whose work was later refined by famed Italian designer Franco Scaglione. George Finley was also in attendance—Finley was Apollo's sales manager in the day. Paula Reisner was also there, widow and partner of Frank Reisner, founder of Intermeccanica, the coachworks in Turin, Italy, that built the bodies for the Apollo GT.

What a fascinating journey! The high point was taking an enthusiastic Milt Brown for a test drive around the boundary road that runs around the Concorso Italiano display area and then engaging in a 45-minute tech session with this wonderful man who had created this car 50 years ago.

Nine years and many thousands of hours later, I have to ask myself, *was it all worth it?*

Absolutely. Was it a barn-find? Yes, the pictures posted on eBay showed the car in a barn. Would I do it again? In a heartbeat! In fact, I have just bought another car built by Intermeccanica, and you guessed it—it was also discovered in a barn!

CHAPTER 44
Leno's Elusive Love

If you're reading this book, of you know that former *Tonight Show* host Jay Leno is a car guy just like the rest of us. Sure, he might have a couple more bucks—and the most famous chin on television—but he likes to follow up leads and make discoveries just like you and me.

Most of Leno's finds have been well documented in my *In The Barn* series of books, such as the Duesenburg he found in a public New York City parking garage, the Gullwing Mercedes 300 SL that had been parked in a storage container, and discovering the "missing" Vincent Black Shadow. But a good car collector or barn-finder is never satisfied, and when people with car stories write him, he follows up with the best.

"People send letters to the studio and tell me about a car they would like to sell, but they want it to

Leno bought this cream-colored beauty 1963 Jaguar E-Type Series I coupe sight unseen.

The storage compartment in the back included the original factory tool bag and the owner's manual.

go to a good home," he says. "They don't want to sell their prized beauty to someone who will profit on it. People know I never sell. They trust that I will care for their cars."

One day, Leno grabbed a handful of letters from the mailbag and came across one from a woman with a message that intrigued him. "This lady wrote me about the 1963 Jaguar E-Type Series I coupe that she purchased new 50 years ago," he says. "She wrote that she once had driven it up to 80 miles-per-hour. And she wanted it to go to a good home."

An E-Type with one-woman ownership and never driven above 80 mph intrigued Leno. He called her and discovered she lived on a huge cattle ranch. And the more she talked, the more interested he became in her car. "I wound up buying it over the phone, sight-unseen," he says. "The car is straight and true, and even the clock and tach work!"

The white coupe with black interior is just what Leno had long hoped for. It has the 3.8-liter engine that he prefers over the later 4.2 liter. It has mostly original paint, and the carpeting and leather interior are factory original.

"We cleaned up the engine compartment, removed the gauges to have them inspected, and changed the shocks," Leno says. "But this car has absolutely no corrosion, even under the floor mats and gas tank."

When he opened the storage compartment in the back, he found the original factory tool bag and the owner's manual. "It was well maintained and driven by a woman, so even the often troublesome Moss gearbox still shifts like new," he says. "It's a car that even Enzo Ferrari said was the best looking car ever, which I believe. I'm so thrilled to own it—it is so much fun to drive."

By the way, the original owner may not have exceeded 80 mph in its first 50 years, but Leno has had it up to 125 mph since purchasing it in early 2013. And how did it feel?

"Like it was brand new," he says, "like it was brand new."

CHAPTER 45

Leno's Voluptuous Vette

Jay Leno has the same reaction to great finds as I do: nothing gets him more stoked than when he discovers another cool old car or bike.

Lucky for me, whenever Leno acquires another barn find, he gets so excited that he calls to tell me about it. Certainly one advantage Leno has is being one of the most visible car collectors in the country, if not the world.

The former host of the *Tonight Show* receives lots of letters from people who want to share stories about their cars. Leno said that he personally reads every letter, usually grabbing a handful from the mailbag on the way to lunch.

"So I grabbed an envelope from a guy in Michigan," he says. "People in Michigan live around cars, so I thought it might be something interesting. The letter said that this man wanted to sell me his

This immaculate 1963 split-window Sting Ray coupe was a car Leno had coveted for a long time.

The odometer on this Sting Ray only reads 991 original miles.

The C-2, or Sting Ray, debuted in 1963, but the split rear window only appeared for one model year.

1963 Fuel-Injected Corvette."

Leno almost choked on his sandwich.

"I've been looking for a fuel-injected Split Window for so long," he says. "But it had to be the right car."

This was the right car. The 1963 Corvette was the first model Sting Ray, known as second generation, or C-2. It was designed by Larry Shinoda with input from Peter Brock and under the direction of Bill Mitchell. At the time, the distinctive sloped rear roof design was a styling breakthrough. However, the rear window was divided by a roof support, which meant the driver had an obstructed view from the inside rear-view mirror.

But despite Father-of-the-Corvette Zora Duntov's protests regarding the rear window design, Mitchell insisted that it remain. And it did for just one year.

Besides being the first Corvette with hide-away headlights and fully independent suspension, 1963 coupes are especially coveted today for their unique rear window styling.

The details of the split window got juicier—the seller said the Vette had just 991 original miles on the odometer!

"The story was that the original owner ordered it, then shipped off to Vietnam," Leno says. "When he got out of the service, he did something that got him in trouble, and he went to prison for 20 years. While he was in the slammer, his grandmother sold the car to a collector, who then sold it to Russ McLean, Corvette Program Manager," he says. "Nobody ever put any miles on it."

Leno explains his Corvette is better that he even hoped for. "It's equipped exactly like I would have ordered one in 1963," he says. "It has power brakes, roll-up windows, and a four-speed."

He had the car inspected by National Corvette Restoration Society (NCRS) members, who confirmed the car's authenticity. "The car is matching-numbers correct, has the correct air cleaner, the correct master cylinder, everything," Leno says.

Leno admits that with only 991 miles on the car, he won't drive it much. But he *is* a car guy, and he drives all his cars. So this car will get a few miles on it from time to time.

"It drives like a brand new car," he says, smiling.

VIII

QUESTIONABLE DESIRES

CHAPTER 46

A British Beauty

Ever since Keith Irwin worked on a customer's Triumph 2000 roadster in his restoration shop a couple of years ago, he knew he had to own one.

An unusual sports car for the day, it was as though Triumph had attempted to build a Rolls Royce sports car rather than a competitor to the MG. "I've worked on British cars for 30 years," Irwin says, "everything from TR2s, TR3s, and TR6s to Austin Healeys and Bug-eye Sprites. I had seen the Triumph 2000 in books, and it was a dream of mine to find one, but never could."

The Triumph 2000 was a special car, although more of touring car than a sports car. Between 1946 and 1949, 4,501 were produced. It was credited as Triumph's first production car after World War II. The standard engine had been used by Jaguar before the war and eventually increased from 1.5 liters to 2 liters. Because of a shortage of steel in postwar Britain, the bodies were made of aluminum. The front fenders were huge, with equally huge headlights and dual horns. And the unique rumble seat had a built-in windshield for passengers.

The Triumph's intricate dashboard is made

Restoration specialist Keith Irwin had heard rumors of a Triumph 2000 Roadster hidden on the North Carolina coast. This is the car's longtime owner as he prepares to help push the car onto Irwin's trailer. KEITH IRWIN

A proud Mr. Irwin with his new acquisition. It's a unique car with a rumble seat, fully wooden dashboard, huge front fenders, headlights, and horns. It is very much more a coach-built car than MGs of the era.
KEITH IRWIN

entirely of red mahogany, instead of wood applied over a metal frame, like many sports cars of its day. The Triumph 2000 appears to be more of a coach-built classic than an assembly line sports car.

Irwin had heard one existed on coastal North Carolina, owned by a gentleman who bought it while in U.S. military service in the Caribbean. The car was imported from England in 1967 by a U.S. sailor, who sold it to the most recent owner in 1970. The gentleman used it on the islands during his time in the service then shipped it back to North Carolina when he was discharged in 1974.

"It sat in this guy's garage for 40 years," Irwin says. "I drove my truck and trailer to his house and wouldn't leave until he sold it to me. The car's black paint job is from 1970, but still looks pretty good."

The 64-year-old car's odometer only reads 23,480 miles. It features right-hand-drive steering and a three-speed transmission. Irwin and his team at Keith Irwin Restorations worked on the car for just two days, flushing the cooling system, rebuilding the brakes, and changing all the fluids, before firing it up.

"He sold me the car with most of the maintenance items I needed," he says. The car features badges from Liverpool, England, the Triumph Roadster Club, and a parking permit from the U.S. Department of the Navy on the island of Antigua.

"When I take it to a car show or a cruise-in, I'm usually hoarse by the time I leave the show because everyone wants me to tell them about it," Irwin says. "Maybe someday I'll restore it, but right now my family and I are enjoying it too much as a survivor."

CHAPTER 47

Unforgettable

John Simmons had never seen one before, had never even heard of an Arnolt Bristol. But when he spotted one on the Virginia Military Institute campus where he was a senior, the car's design made the engineering student weak in the knees.

Soon thereafter, the car was posted on a bulletin board for sale by another VMI student who needed the money for graduate school. Simmons's time had come.

Simmons was already a British car enthusiast; he counted a Triumph TR4 as his daily driver. But this Arnolt Bristol was something he had to own. The fact that it had a modified Chevy 283 engine and GM three-speed gearbox didn't faze him. So he borrowed the $1,100 asking price from his father and made plans to pick it up during the 1968 Thanksgiving holiday.

"So my brother and me loaded up the TR4 and started on the 200-mile drive from Lexington, Virginia to White Stone," says Simmons, 66, from Charlotte, North Carolina. "But the Triumph jumped a timing chain and stopped running. Fortunately my aunt lived near where we broke down, so we borrowed her Buick and towed the broken TR4 to her house," he says. (The TR4 stayed there through the following summer.) "Then we used her Buick to pick up the Arnolt."

John Simmons bought this rare Arnolt Bristol in 1968 from a student who needed to sell it for graduate school tuition. The Chevy-powered car was a daily driver before being locked away for 40 years. TOM COTTER

Arnolt Bristols have an interesting history. Stanley "Wacky" Arnolt, a Chicago businessman and sports car enthusiast, purchased driving chassis from Bristol Cars, Ltd., in England, and had them shipped to Bertone in Italy, where they were wrapped in an attractive (if edgy) steel body. The cars were powered by the 130-horsepower, six-cylinder Bristol engine, which was designed before World War II for use in both airplanes and the BMW 328 sports car.

The Arnolt Bristol's body seems tall and sits high on its chassis. Designer Franco Scaglione (who would also design the Alfa Romeo BAT series) had to work around the tall Bristol chassis and engine combination.

A total of 142 Arnolt Bristols were manufactured between 1953 and 1958, including 136 roadsters and 6 coupes. They were marketed as an American car and sold through Arnolt's headquarters in Chicago. Simmons's Bristol has serial number 3071, which translates to the 71st model manufactured.

The cars came in three models: a stripped racing model, the Bolide, and the Deluxe. The Bolide was well appointed with necessities, but the Deluxe featured luxury items such as door handles, an instrument pod, door panels, and side windows.

Despite racing successes at Sebring and other events, the cars never sold well. Today, only about 85 exist in varying conditions. Simmons's car, after being used as a daily driver for about eight years, has sat obediently in his garage for almost the last four decades.

But that hibernation is about to end, and a rejuvenation is about to begin. "I plan to keep it looking unrestored, but because the original engines are so expensive, I'll either keep the Chevy in it, or replace it with a GM V-6 or a Volvo B-20," he says. "It will look original, but be more affordable."

CHAPTER 48
Carriage–House Creeping

Let's face it—if people know you are into old vehicles, you'll be the first to know when friends and acquaintances hear about old cars and bikes. This scenario played out recently when a friend of Michael DePalo's, Rob Engle, stopped by his shop and told him about a woman he worked with.

People know DePalo is into both cars and bikes. He has an incredibly restored American Motors AMX in his home garage and has restored a number of very cool old trucks.

And by being one of Long Island's Royal Enfield motorcycle dealers, DePalo sometimes hears about bike finds as well. One of his best Royal Enfield customers, in fact, is his friend and music legend, Billy Joel.

"This woman had an old motorcycle in her carriage house that she wanted to get rid of so she could do some remodeling," Engle told DePalo, who lives in Bayport, New York. "The bike had been sitting for so long that the wheels were frozen up and wouldn't roll."

So DePalo called the woman, Janet, who asked him to come over to see if he would be interested in the bike. She gave him directions to her Deer Park home, but mistakenly told him to go north when she meant south.

"My son, Zack, and I were driving and driving," DePalo says. "It was like we were on one of those barn-find television shows where the guys get lost. So I called Janet and she finally gave me the correct directions."

Longer Islander Michael DePalo was asked to look at an old motorcycle in a woman's carriage house. It turned out to be a low-mileage Norton in restorable condition. MICHAEL DEPALO

When the DePalos arrived, Janet showed him and his son the bike and told them the story. Janet's husband had owned the bike, a 1975 Norton Commando MK III Electric Start. He had purchased the bike in the late 1970s from Ghost Motorcycle in Port Washington, New York.

The bike only had 5,800 miles on the odometer, and the last inspection sticker was issued in 1977. Janet's husband was in the process of repairing the bike, because the side cover was removed and the transmission was partly disassembled. When he died in 1983, all work on the bike stopped. When their son didn't express interest in the bike, it just sat on the dirt floor from 1983 until DePalo hauled it out 30 years later.

"It was pretty much all there," he says. "There was a small bag of parts, but the kick starter was missing. So we started digging in the dirt, and there it was! The brakes were frozen; probably just the disc pucks frozen to the rotor. So I just sprayed some penetrating oil between the caliper and the rotor, and they loosened right up."

DePalo says all the paint is checked and peeling, but the inside of the gas tank was dry and rust-free. "I'm not quite sure what I'm going to do with the bike yet, but my 14-year-old son, Zack, is pretty excited about it. It might be a good first bike for him."

And maybe he, too, will catch the barn-find bug.

CHAPTER 49

Having Your Way With A Vixen

by Mitch Goldstein

W hile visiting an artist's studio in Lancaster, South Carolina, I spotted on the wall in a corner what was obviously a European wood-rimmed steering wheel from the '60s. "Forget about your artwork," I said, "tell me where that wheel came from."

He couldn't remember the name of the car, but that it began with a "T." It had a tube chassis and fiberglass body. He thought it may have been a kit car. The odd thing he said, though, was that it had two rear shocks on each side.

"TVR?" I asked him.

Bingo.

The artist hadn't seen the car for about 20 years. When he last drove it, it had been overheating and experiencing electrical problems. He parked it in a garage for nine years, then gave it to his son and a friend to "fix up." It went to the friend's property in Lancaster, where it sat outside for the next 11 years.

The artist gave me the name of his son's friend. I found a couple of numbers on the Internet. He answered the first number I called.

A sad scene, for sure. This TVR Vixen had languished in the outdoors for many years before Goldstean was able to negotiate its purchase. Surprisingly, with a new battery and some starter fluid, the engine fired to life!

MITCH GOLDSTEIN

Goldstein restores cars mechanically but loves to leave their cosmetics as found, so he's been making the scene at the local Cars & Coffee cruise-ins with his rolling barn-find. MITCH GOLDSTEIN

It was about a 45-minute drive from my house to their property. It seemed like it was in the middle of nowhere. I met him in the rain outside of what was his grandparent's house. We walked around the side of the house, down a muddy slope and past some goat pens. As we walked toward it, all I could see was the top of the roof sticking up between a large rusty machine lathe and a pile of car parts. A dead flatbed truck blocked it from the front.

The 1968 Vixen sat on blocks, but I remember seeing the wheels at the art studio along with the steering wheel. The engine was covered with the hood from another car even though the hood that belonged with the TVR sat in the weeds a few feet away. The radiator lay under the car, and the headlight assemblies were in the engine compartment.

I returned within the week, mounted new tires, got the car on the ground, and hauled it home. If it wasn't one of only 117 Series I Vixens made (VX199F), you would take one look at it and call it a parts car. It had been running when parked, but the engine was still free, so I dropped a battery in it and cranked it over. After a couple of minutes of cranking, the oil pressure came up.

My son sat in the car and cranked some more while I sprayed starting fluid in the frozen carb. It fired up! The floodgates opened. I rebuilt the hydraulics, brakes, fuel, and cooling systems.

But will I ever restore it? Right now, it's tough to say. I'm still having too much fun driving it to tear it down for a lengthy restoration.

But talk to me in a couple of years—we'll see if we can reach a deal!

CHAPTER 50

Looking for Tin Lizzy

Ken Trout had given up on ever finding a Model T Tudor sedan.

He had already owned two Model T roadsters—one steel, and the other fiberglass, both which he converted to hot rods—but the much-sought two-door sedan would remain elusive.

Trout had paid his dues in all forms of the automotive business. The 64-year-old moved from Tennessee to Charlotte, North Carolina—NASCAR country— and in the 1960s went to work for Harry Hyde's K & K Insurance NASCAR team, which fielded cars for driver Bobby Isaac.

For the next 30 years, Trout stayed in Charlotte, working for various race teams. During his free time, he built hot rods and dragsters. In the 1980s, he also built a 1949 VW Beetle, one of the earliest Volkswagen resto-rods.

In his time, Trout had built every hot car he desired, except one—the Model T sedan. "I always wanted one, but could never find a two-door sedan," Trout says, who today lives in Lebanon, Tennessee.

Until, that is, he *did* find one.

He was walking through the AutoFair swap meet at Charlotte Motor Speedway a few years ago, and there, on a trailer, sat his dream car—a 1925 Ford Tudor. "It had been sitting in a Georgia barn for 64 years," Trout says.

The original owner decided to restore his trusty old Ford and started to dismantle it. The fenders, running boards, hood, and radiator were removed.

After a long search, Ken Trout of Lebanon, Tennessee, finally found a Model T Ford Tudor sedan. It was basically a one-owner when he bought it. KEN TROUT

Trout simply lifted the body up, sold the original frame and drivetrain, and rolled this new Hemi-powered chassis underneath. The car has a very modified drivetrain, but the body still has the black paint from 1925! KEN TROUT

"But then he got real sick," Trout says, "and all work stopped."

The car was parked near an open door in a barn on the original owner's property, causing people to regularly inquire whether the car was for sale. So the owner's relatives covered the car with a tarp and let it sit for decades. When the owner died, the family held an estate sale and sold the Model T Ford sedan to an old car enthusiast in Georgia.

"When I saw it at Charlotte, I bought it on the spot," Trout says. He removed the body and sold off the original chassis, which included the engine, transmission, rear differential, and suspension. Then he built a custom chassis, and working with his 10-year-old nephew, Eugene, installed a modified 392 Chrysler Hemi engine, which was left over from Trout's old nostalgia dragster. The pair also installed a four-speed road racing gearbox, narrowed 9-inch Ford rear, and a racing fuel cell. "I built it basically as a street-legal A-Altered drag race car," he says.

But lest you think that with the car's powerful drivetrain and racing pedigree that it also has a slick black paint job that appears to be 6 inches deep, better think again.

"I didn't touch the original paint," Trout says. "It didn't have any rust, so I left the original black paint. It just looks great with all that patina."

IX

DAMAGED GOODS

CHAPTER 51

The Ugliest Woody

When I dragged this ugly vehicle into my neighborhood, I know my neighbors could sense their real estate values plunging. To be sure, this thing is ugly, possibly one of the ugliest I've ever dragged home.

But it's also rare. And has a great story.

From the time this Ford left the dealership in 1947, it has lived in one town its whole life: Maggie Valley, North Carolina. The family who bought the Woody when it was new—yes, Woody—owned a small ski area in the resort mountain town. In the 1940s, ski lifts were expensive and exotic pieces of equipment, so someone in the family came up with a brilliant idea: they would order a Ford Woody wagon from the local dealership with a rare and expensive option—a Marmon-Herrington Four Wheel Drive system.

What could I possibly see in it? My wife asks the same thing. Actually, the car/truck is desirable simply for its rare Marmon-Herrington 4X4 drivetrain. This one was once a ski lift! MARK COUGHLIN

This vehicle will never be restored, but it's 4X4 system will be moved to another car one day.

The ski area operator drove skiers up the hill in the 4x4 Woody, and they skied down!

The Marmon-Herrington system was cumbersome and expensive, doubling the price of a standard Woody wagon from the dealership. But it was the best all-terrain system of the day. Decades later, after the Woody had been used up as a ski lift, the harsh winters had taken their toll on the wooden body. It had rotted badly.

The original owners sold their sad old Woody to another local resident who removed the wood and welded a modified Ford truck cab onto the 1947 passenger car nose, and mounted a 3/4-ton pick-up box in the back. The same owner continued to use the vehicle for many more years in and around Maggie Valley.

By the time the second owner parked his Marmon-Herrington for good, local car and motorcycle collector (and picker extraordinaire) Steve Davis was there with cash in hand. Davis bought the odd Woody/truck and drove it to his storage yard, where it sat for a couple of decades.

Then I showed up—driving a 1939 Ford Deluxe Woody wagon I bought when I was 15 years old, no less—and Steve mentions that he has a Marmon-Herrington Woody.

The axles were frozen up and the steering column was locked, so a tractor was employed to help load this find onto the trailer.

"Have you ever heard of a Marmon-Herrington?" he asked.

"Have I heard of Marmon-Herrington? I have owned two of them over the past few years!" I said.

Davis was shocked. He said that since I was a real Woody guy, he'd sell me the car if I was interested.

So I bought it, and now I'm struggling on what to do next. The drivetrain is rare, but the chassis is rusty and the body is junk. So I'll likely strip off the fabricated body and sell it to some rat-rodder.

Lucky for me, though, I own another '47 Ford Woody body that I'll mount on there. It will be a lengthy and expensive restoration when the cost of a new wooden body is considered, so I'll most likely sell or trade the rare 4x4 Woody to someone with more woodworking talent than me.

But I couldn't pass up a vehicle with a great story like the 4x4 ski lift—could you?

CHAPTER 52

The Squalid Squatter Chicken Poop Convertible

Mark Elliott became acquainted with the old Porsche over the Thanksgiving holiday in 1972. The asking price was $1,500, and it was sitting in a Kansas City chicken coop.

When Elliot arrived there, it was very cold. He looked at the car—a 1959 Convertible D—and turned his nose up a bit. The car looked and smelled pretty rough—that's what happens when something spends years inside a chicken coop. Soon, Elliott was invited into the owner's house for a drink.

"Son, I don't want to take advantage of you," the owner said. "I'll take $900 for the car."

The price was right, though it took Elliott a while to de-poop the damn thing; at the time, he was just a young college student. "I'd been through eight or nine Porsche 356s at that point," he says. "The cars were considered obsolete. We drove that convertible in snow storms with the top down because it was so cold that the back window would have cracked if we tried to assemble it." Following graduation, he bought a 911.

Even though Elliott moved to Florida in 1974, restoration on the convertible began in Missouri. The white car was to be repainted in black lacquer, but halfway through the process, the restorer was killed in an auto accident.

It went from bad to worse: Mark Elliott bought this Porsche covered in chicken poop, drove the piss out of it, then parked it in his uncle's hanger and covered it with pesticides to keep the rats out! MARK ELLIOTT

Elliott figured 42 years of hibernation were enough, so he dragged the rare convertible out of the hanger and to his Florida home for restoration. Hopefully.
MARK ELLIOTT

The unfinished hulk and all its components were towed into Elliott's uncle's nearby airplane hangar, where it was covered with pesticides so rats wouldn't take over (just don't tell the EPA). The little Porsche was pushed into a corner and forgotten.

For the next 42 years.

During that time, Elliott's uncle used every opportunity to remind his nephew that the car was still sitting in his hanger. "A tornedo came through the area a few years ago and damaged the barn, exposing the car to the elements," he says. By 2013, enough time had elapsed, so Elliott hooked his trailer up to his truck and made the long trek from St. Petersburg, Florida, to Missouri, to pick up his long-idled Porsche project.

By this time, Elliott had become known as the Porsche Gypsy. At one time, he once owned 37 Porsche 356s that at one time or another had all sat in a field behind his house. "Believe it or not, I once found a 1955 Porsche 550 Spyder during a snow storm," he says.

Of the convertible, Elliot says, "It was like my '59 convertible had been slumbering all those years, just waiting for me to get working on it." The Porsche has matching numbers, and because it was stored in a dry hangar with a concrete floor for four decades, the tub was still in good condition. Elliott said the car is complete down to every nut and bolt and top bow, and the pesticides had certainly helped keep the rat and mouse damage to a minimum.

"I still need to decide whether to complete the restoration that I started in 1974, or sell the car," he says. "This Porsche is like a time capsule. And it's been preserved with Missouri mud, which could be the best preservative known to man!"

CHAPTER 53
The Pawn Broker In The Bush

by Somer Hooker

In 2008, I went to an estate sale in Columbia, Tennessee, where 30 cars were advertised. As I approached the sale, I was greeted by a Rolls Royce that had been outside for a while. Next to it was an early '50s Studebaker torpedo nose. I then spied a large hut that would typically be used for storing farm equipment. Inside, a crowd had gathered around a 1977 Pontiac Trans Am with only 2,800 miles. Across from it was a Plymouth Road Runner with the rare reflective side trim. A few feet away, however, things went downhill: a 1959 Corvette with 69,000 miles had spent time too much time outside and was still doing duty as a leaf composter. The top had long ago collapsed and filled with leaves. A

DeLorean also rested nearby with a healthy scrim of *mold* growing on the inside.

I was ill prepared for the neglect I found when I walked out back. Here sat numerous cars in various states of decay. More once-upon-a-time "cherry" cars were now the pits. A one-owner 1956 Chevrolet Bel Air had been left to rot; as the fenders rusted, the rearview mirrors just fell off. Another Trans Am had been left with one window open so a dog could get in.

As I looked around, I would see a vehicle that appeared to be OK from a distance, but as I got closer, I saw that the windows had been left down, allowing the floorboards to rot along with the interior. A driver's feet could go through the floor a la Fred Flintstone.

Resembling an automotive Jurassic Park, barn-finder Somer Hooker once attended a depressing estate sale where low mileage cars like this 2,800-mile, 1977 Pontiac Firebird, lay wasted. SOMER HOOKER

Some convertibles had fought the valiant fight; as their tops deteriorated, cheap green tarps had been thrown over them, only to wind up as rotted green threads. Other vehicles had become trash dumps for records and files. Anything with a nonferrous structure became a mold colony: Bricklins, Corvettes, and Avantis slowly started "greening," if you may.

Further back, another shed exposed even more horrors; the cement block building had a collapsed roof. Tool boxes that sat open filled with water and rusted through. Insulation falling down provided a bit of "frosting" on the cake. There was a once pristine 'Cuda in there—under the hood, mice had filled the engine compartment with winter rations, and the vinyl bucket seats had deteriorated. Underneath was the skeleton of a rat. But even so, the family did not want to sell the car—some speculated that maybe it wasn't "ripe" enough.

For years each autumn, people could see these cars from the highway. The owner was constantly besieged by passersby wanting to buy, but he always refused. Many speculated that he came across these vehicles from his longtime lucrative pawn business. Other cars, though, had been inherited from family members or bought on a whim. They all became a time study in decay.

The Corvette was sold for $65,000. The Roadrunner sold for $20,000, and the '56 Bel Air for $4,000. The low-mileage Trans Am brought $28,000.

They were all pawns in the end.

Cars with windows left open and mold growing inside were commonplace. This once pristine 'Cuda had the skeleton of a rat underneath. SOMER HOOKER

CHAPTER 54

Time Capsule Dealership

At one time, Robert Collier owned a thriving American Motors dealership in rural North Carolina. It had been started by his grandfather as a wagon dealership sometime in the late 1800s, then sold Willys Overland, Studebaker, and Whippet vehicles.

When Collier's father took over the business, he sold Nash and Rambler vehicles. When Collier inherited the business from his father, the AMC dealership was thriving as it supplied local residents with Matadors, Rebels, Americans, and the occasional Javelin and AMX.

Then in 1980, something happened in the auto industry that shook Collier's world; the French company Renault purchased a large share of AMC in order to bring much-needed capital to their manufacturing operations. "I'd been a Rambler and American Motors dealership since the 1950s," Collier says, in his late 80s. "But I just closed down when American Motors was purchased by the French. I wasn't going to sell none of them Renaults."

An 8-foot tall cyclone fence was installed around the property, a padlock was installed on the gate, and the time capsule began. Today, more than three decades later, the dealership still sits virtually untouched.

In the showroom, racks are still stocked with colorful brochures showing new 1979 AMC products that were then on the market. Two AMXs sit in the

Robert Collier moves among the relics inside the once stylish showroom of Collier Motors in Pikeville, North Carolina, which now sits forlorn and neglected. It contains two rare AMX two-seaters, a Packard sedan, an Ambassador convertible, and a few motorcycles. Roof leaks have caused the ceiling tiles to fall down on the cars.
TOM COTTER

What was once a used car lot is now overgrown and nearly impassable. More than 250 cars are still parked in rows on the property, but many—especially the convertibles—have trees growing right through their bodies.
TOM COTTER

showroom, and the parts department is still stocked with NOS water pumps, distributor caps, and brake shoes. Collier and his son, Rob, still repair the occasional AMC product for old customers in their well-equipped service bays.

The most *Jurassic Park*–like scene is what was formerly Collier's used car lot: when the dealership closed down, at least 250 cars sat on the mowed lawn. But that lawn went unmowed, and acorns turned into small bushes that became small trees. Today, a forest exists where the used lot once sat; huge trees grow through what were once Matador and American convertibles, like the cars were somehow lowered by helicopter from the heavens over these maple trees.

Hundreds of cars litter the forest, including some very unusual examples: 390-cubic-inch AMXs, a bevy of Nash Healey sports cars, the personal AMX of late Arizona Senator Barry Goldwater (complete with custom aircraft gauges that were installed courtesy of your tax dollars!).

These are just a few of the cars that are returning to the earth, deteriorating badly after decades of sitting outside in winter cold, summer heat, flooding rains, and parching drought.

Collier's AMC could be the American version of the famous French barn-find collection, which was discovered 30 years ago. Called Sleeping Beauties, these interesting and rare cars were left for decades to literally rot into the earth. It was also the discovery that made this author realize that there might be some amazing cars still hidden out there. That is when I began to think about writing barn-find books like this.

Is it a sin that Robert Collier lets these cars deteriorate?

"Everything is for sale," he says when I asked him if I could purchase a rapidly deteriorating Nash Healey coupe. "You know, these sell for at least two-hundred thousand dollars."

Sure, I thought, *exactly ten times what a car of this condition is valued.*

CHAPTER 55
The Sneak-A-Peek Scooter

I t was a typical Saturday morning for Michael Blackburn. He was hanging out with friends at the local coffee shop, Diamonds, and talking about motorcycles.

One of Blackburn's friends, Steve Doeden— knowing that Blackburn already owned one motor scooter—asked Doeden if he might be interested in owning another. One of Doeden's neighbors had told Blackburn that Doeden and his siblings rode an Italian scooter around the yard as kids, but when they got older, it was parked in his mother's garden shed. Decades later, it was still there.

"I really didn't want another scooter," Blackburn says. "But the 'Guy Rule' dictates that I must at least put an eyeball on it." So the following weekend, Blackburn followed his GPS to Doeden's mom's house, about 20 miles away.

"After the snow blower, lawn mower, and other yard implements were removed, the scooter was revealed," he says. "It was in a sorry state. Parts were scattered around, the rear tire was dry rotted, the front was flat, the cast iron center kickstand was broken, and the tool box was a mouse condo. We dragged it outside where it saw the light of day for the first time in 36 years."

But the sunshine didn't help; it was still pretty rough. Blackburn identified it as a 1958 Lambretta 150Ld that "ran when parked." Blackburn really wanted to take a pass on the scooter, though, so he offered the woman $100, hoping to get back into

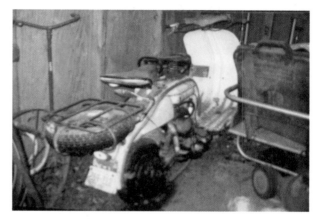

Michael Blackburn didn't want to buy the scooter, a 1958 Lambretta. But the "Guy Rule" dictated that he at least look at it before saying no. When he saw this wreck of a bike, he still managed to say, "Yes, I'll take it." MICHAEL BLACKBURN

his warm truck without violating the "Guy Rule." Problem was, she accepted his offer.

Blackburn was sunk; he didn't want the scooter because he had too many other projects at the same time. Plus, he didn't have room for it. When his friend Bob Steck offered his heated garage for storage, Blackburn crafted a plan; he would restore the scooter and present it to his wife at a Father's Day event in eight months.

The next weekend, Blackburn and Steck hosed off the Lambretta and removed the mouse condo. They removed the spark plug and discovered the engine produced spark. Sourcing parts from the

He restored the scooter in a "Mod" British motif and presented it to his wife, Colleen, as a surprise. It runs and rides great. MICHAEL BLACKBURN

United States, England, India, and Israel, Blackburn replaced tires, tubes, exhaust, and cables, and rebuilt the carburetor.

On a chilly February day, Blackburn filled the fuel tank with fresh fuel, pushed it down the driveway, popped the clutch, and the engine fired up! He rode it around the block, trying to avoid wiping out on ice and snow in the street.

With spray paint from Ace Hardware and reflective tape, Blackburn decided on an Austin Powers–type, Union Jack paint job for the scooter's side panels because that was all the style in the 1960s.

As Father's Day approached, Blackburn was pressed for time, but he was still able to get a license plate with his wife's name: Colleen. "The scooter still needed a couple of things fixed, but it made the big unveil under its own power with family and friends watching," Blackburn says. She was completely surprised," he remembers, "I was a god . . . for about an hour!"

CHAPTER 56

Into The Woods:
The Abandoned Lead-Sled

Because Jason Skufca was 14 years old, he quickly became bored during his parent's trip to a local Ohio Vineyard in 1986.

"After about an hour of watching grownups enjoying accordion music and cheese samples, I got bored," Skufca says. So he decided to explore the vineyard grounds and surrounding woods.

He soon forgot his boredom. He found an abandoned and collapsed house deep in the woods, and behind it a collapsed garage. From a distance, he saw a glimpse of a red fender and a wide-white-wall tire. He ran to the opening and realized it was a 1950 Mercury.

"My grandfather had given me a stack of old custom car magazines," he says. "I was obsessed with customizers George and Sam Barris."

The car was in sad shape; it had been parked on a wooden floor, which had rotted, so the car had sunk into the ground. Part of the garage rafters had collapsed, and they were gently resting on the car's roof, though they hadn't done too much damage. "The house's chimney had fallen over and the bricks damaged one door pretty hard," Skufca says. "And there was no interior except for a rotted front seat."

But when he opened the hood, he realized that this was not just a stock Mercury; in place of the original

The hot rod Mercury had once been in a shed, but that building had long since fallen down when Jason Skufca stumbled upon the custom car at the abandoned homesite.
JASON SKUFCA

To his credit, Skufca held onto the car since discovering the 1950 Merc in 1986. Little by little, he is restoring the car to its lead sled roots. JASON SKUFCA

flathead V-8 sat a "nail-head" Buick engine. And the emblems had been shaved from the hood. "This was a mild custom that had just been abandoned," Skufca says.

He hurried back to the winery and told his father of his discovery. After verifying his son's story, Skufca's father asked the winery owners about the car. "The Merc had belonged to the vineyard owner's brother," Skufca says, "and they said the house, garage, and car was to be plowed over by a bulldozer in the near future."

For the Skufcas, that just wasn't acceptable. So they made a quick call to the brother, and a $50 purchase was finalized. The real challenge now was removing the car since the house and garage had collapsed around it, and many trees had grown since the car was parked there decades earlier.

"My father loaded tools, sledgehammers, saws, and chains into his Jeep," he says. "We removed the rear wall of the garage and after cutting down several trees, chained the Mercury to the Jeep and pulled it out backward into a nearby field."

Later that week, they hired a flatbed truck to pick up the car and deliver it to the Skufca house. "In 1986, old lead-sleds were not as popular in Ohio as they were on the West Coast," Skufca says. "It was just a rotted old car and people pretty much thought we were nuts."

Over the years, Skufca shuffled the Mercury from one storage building to another. But even though he's had many offers to sell, he and his father have slowly been working on the car. The rotted floors have been replaced, along with much of the lower half of the body.

"We installed a new drivetrain and chopped the top," he says. "I will never forget that summer. I felt like an explorer who just stumbled upon an undiscovered tomb."

CHAPTER 57

The Dentist, Angie's List, And One Rough Porsche

Don Fowler was sitting in the dentist's chair as the dentist poked and prodded around the inside of his mouth when the dentist—a fellow car enthusiast—told him he had just inspected an old Porsche Cabriolet.

"He told me it was pretty rough," says Fowler, of Summerfield, North Carolina. "He said he wanted nothing to do with it. He said I could have it if I wanted it." So Fowler got the seller's information and inspected it himself.

"I've been fooling with Porsches for 40 years and I've never seen one so eaten up underneath," he says. Besides being in poor condition, the 1958 "Normal" Cabriolet was also disassembled. Regardless, Fowler bought the car and spent a month bolting it back together.

The silver Porsche had a black hardtop, black interior, and tan rubber floor mats. "I try to find out the history of my cars," he says. "The original owner was an Air Force pilot stationed in Germany.

The Porsche's original owner drove the car through Cherokee, North Carolina, decades earlier and had a photo taken with an Indian. Porsche used that photo in a calendar and Fowler has had the photo on his wall for 30 years!
DON FOWLER COLLECTION

Finding a barn-find Porsche doesn't happen too often in the dentist chair, but Don Fowler's dentist was a car guy as well. He asked Fowler if he might be interested in a rusty convertible, Fowler said, "Uh huh." DON FOWLER

He bought the car from the factory and met Ferry Porsche on delivery. He shipped the car to New York and drove it home to Texas."

On the way, he stopped in Cherokee, North Carolina, and took a photograph of the Porsche with an Indian. He sent that photo to Porsche, who later used it for a calendar. "Coincidentally I've had that photo hanging on my wall for 30 years," Fowler says. "What are the chances of that?!"

Deciding it was too much for him to restore, Fowler posted the car on eBay. It was listed for a week,

and jumped $20,000 in the last six seconds—certainly something to smile about, and to thank the dentist for the kind referral.

Fowler later learned who bought the Porsche. It was the CEO of Angie's List, an online website for good referrals. From the dentist to Fowler to the new CEO, the next owner could possibly be you—but you'll need a good referral!

X

BABY COME BACK

CHAPTER 58
Dad's Snakecharming TR4

Tom Richardson Sr.'s 1963 Triumph TR4 wasn't quite new when he bought it from Jack Wagner. According to his son, Tommy, now 54, his dad sold the MGTC and bought the Triumph. Tommy's mother drove a 1959 Chevy station wagon, so the TR4 became Tom Sr.'s daily driver in the North Carolina mountains for several years.

"He made a little jumpseat for me and my sister," Tommy says, "and he installed a luggage rack. The

The Richardson's TR4 "back in the day." This is the car that brought the family to races at Virginia International Raceway and hillclimbs at Chimney Rock. Tom Richardson sold the car to a local enthusiast in 1971. T. O. RICHARDSON

whole family would go on trips to places like VIR (Virginia International Raceway), and the Chimney Rock Hillclimb. My father always read *Road & Track* magazine and followed Formula One in the 1960s. As a kid, he always bought me the newest Matchbox Grand Prix cars."

Eventually, though, negotiating the heavy winter snows in the car became a real chore, so he sold the Triumph in 1971 to Bob Thompson and bought a first-generation 4x4 Ford Bronco.

"That Triumph wasn't worth a crap in the snow," says Tommy Jr.

Thompson used the TR4 sparingly, but parked it in 1973 when he went into the military, fully expecting to come home again to enjoy the peppy little sports car on western North Carolina's mountain roads. "He removed the wheels and put them in the basement of his mother's house, and drained all the fluids," Tommy says. "He did a meticulous job of storing the car."

But after his tour of duty, Thompson instead moved to Alaska and left the Triumph to languish in a shed in his mother's backyard for decades.

Tommy Richardson, meanwhile, just assumed the Triumph had been in Alaska with Thompson all these years, but by accident, he discovered that his father's old sports car was still in North Carolina, where it had sat since 1973.

"I decided to buy it in 1999 and surprise my dad for his 67th birthday," Tommy says. "The original paint compounded out like new, and once I added fluids, the car started right up. As it was sitting there running, a big old snake stuck his head out from the

All it needed was fluids and some lubrication.

heater vent. If I had been driving the car, I would have jumped out."

Tommy used ether to chase the black snake from its long-time habitat before he presented his father with the car. "The leather seats deteriorated when you touched them, and the carpets were rotted, but otherwise, it was like a time capsule," Tommy says. "We had a little birthday party and I told him, 'Dad, your birthday present is downstairs.' It looked so good—he just loved it."

Unfortunately, Tom Richardson passed away not long afterward in 2008, and he never had a chance to again enjoy his pride-and-joy on the road. His son covered the car up in the garage, left his father's tools where they were, and turned out the light.

"It's sitting in a building and I haven't touched it since he passed," Tommy says.

When the car was discovered in 1999, it was cleaned up by his children and presented as a surprise to Tom Richardson for his 67th birthday.

CHAPTER 59
Pleasing Daddy

In 1965, Deb Sanders's father, Pete, did what many 28-year-olds wish they could have done: he went to Lynch-Davidson Motors, the local Ford dealer in Jacksonville, Florida, and bought a new GT-350 Mustang. The car was delivered with steel wheels and without stripes (though he and some friends painted the stripes in the driveway soon after bringing it home).

Shelby #5S545 became the family car, with Deb's mom driving the car for shopping, dropping the kids at school, and whatever errands needed to be run. It became necessary to install a rear seat when they took the car to upstate New York for vacations. They also installed an air conditioner.

In 1973, the Shelby was stolen from a downtown Jacksonville parking lot and recovered two weeks later, minus the drivetrain. Disgruntled and upset, Pete began collecting parts and disassembled the car for restoration, which was never completed.

He signed the title over to Deb—who was five when he purchased the car—in 2010. Deb became very involved in the car's reassembly, along with her friend, Phil Murphy. Rather than restoring the car, Deb decided to reassemble the car with as many original parts as possible. The result is a GT-350 with all the character and comfort of a used pair of blue jeans.

In the middle of this work, Deb moved from Florida to New York to Maryland. "It's amazing

A young Deb Saunders poses next to her dad's 1966 Shelby Mustang GT-350. The car provided her family with daily driver chores until it was stolen in 1973. When returned, it was minus the drivetrain. Restored, it is now one of the most popular cars at National Shelby meets. DEB SAUNDERS

that we were only missing a few parts when it was assembled," she says.

Deb enjoys the attention the car brings when she attends Shelby American Automobile Club (SAAC) conventions.

CHAPTER 60

Grandma Betty's Secret

To condense this story down to a few hundred words is an injustice; it could easily be a book itself!

Zach Straits, who grew up in Ohio, discovered when he was 12 years old that he was adopted in California as an infant. His adoptive parents died when Straits was young, and while rummaging through some family paperwork after their deaths, he discovered his adoption papers.

Years later, when a friend invited Straits to accompany him to California on a business trip, he gladly accepted, thinking that it might be an opportunity to investigate his family roots. While there, he

Grandma Betty proudly shows off her Camaro. With her are husband, Bob, and son, Greg. ZACH STRAITS

Straits discovered his Grandmother's Camaro behind the family home in Kingman, Arizona. The car was in surprisingly good condition.
ZACH STRAITS

Straits and his wife, Brenda, have been enjoying the Camaro, displaying it as-is at shows until they dive into a full-blown restoration.
ZACH STRAITS

began to investigate the whereabouts of his birth mother by researching at both the LA Public Library and the Mormon Library. And through his exhaustive work, he determined his mother's full name through LA County marriage records.

To cut a long and wonderful story short, Straits also discovered he had a brother and a sister. After a brief Internet search, he discovered that his brother, Greg, lived in Kingman, Arizona, so he drove there, where he met his mother and half-brother. It would be several months later that he found his sister, Suzy, and her family in Oregon.

His newly found relatives began telling Straits stories about his Grandma Betty. "She was the original little old lady from Pasadena," Straits says, who was about to discover that his grandmother loved fast cars as much as he did. "In 1967, she wanted a fast car to drive to work, so she went to Courtesy Chevrolet in Los Angeles and special-ordered a new Camaro."

Then Straits' mother jumped in: "It's covered up in the backyard right now!" she said.

As a certified barn-finder, sweat started running down the back of Straits' neck. He ran outside, lifted the cover, and discovered it was an SS/RS with automatic, bench seat, air conditioning, tinted windows, and a 350 with 295 horsepower.

"In the desert, it was hard to tell that the valve covers and air cleaner were chrome because of all the dust," he says. He also discovered a couple of speeding tickets from the same cop in the same month and was told that Grandma Betty regularly "caught air" over LA railroad tracks. It had been parked since 1984.

Sadly, Straits' mother passed away from cancer, but the children promised her the Camaro would stay in the family and in original condition. Together, the family decided that Straits, who has performed several body-off, nut-and-bolt restorations, would eventually restore the car and enjoy it for a period of time. Until then, though, he's enjoying the Camaro as-is.

"She's already been a big hit at local car shows in its desert-find condition," he says. It was also decided that since neither he nor his brother, Greg, have children, he'd eventually send the car to his sister Suzy's family in Oregon for her children to enjoy.

CHAPTER 61
Harry's Curious Cunningham

With only 25 Cunningham C-3s ever built, it's amazing that one appears in this barn-find book. For that matter, it's even more amazing that *two* barn-find Cunningham stories appear here.

Classic car sleuth Chuck Schoendorf, of Rowayton, Connecticut—the owner of a terrific collection of cars, including two Cunninghams—was on the lookout for C-3 #5209, the fourth built between 1952 and 1953 out of a run of 25 at the Cunningham factory in West Palm Beach, Florida.

Number 5209 was the only missing Cunningham C-3, which after more than 60 years is amazing in

Harry Sefried drove his Cunningham C-3 with abandon when he bought it in the early 1960s. He even bought speed parts directly from Briggs Cunningham. But then he parked the car in his backyard, where it sat for decades. TOM COTTER

itself. In 2011, Schoendorf made it his mission to either find the car or find out why it no longer existed.

Records show that the car was last owned by a Mr. Harry Sefried Jr. of Connecticut. Obituary archives showed Mr. Sefried died in 2005, but the obituary did not mention where he resided. It did, however, mention a daughter named Leslie Lockhard.

Schoendorf investigated and discovered that a Leslie Lockhard lived in Pennsylvania, and — BINGO!—there it was. "Yes, I still own the car, and it is still sitting behind my father's house in Connecticut," she said, rather surprised about the phone call. "But it's probably in pretty rough condition. It's been sitting outside for at least fifteen years."

Since the elderly Sefried was wheelchair-bound, he had kept the car in the backyard rather than in the nearby empty garage, so he could keep an eye on it out of the window of his house.

As a younger man, Sefried had a wild streak. He raced motorcycles, and when he purchased the C-3 in 1962, he purchased high-compression pistons, a high-lift camshaft, larger valves, and roller-tappets directly from Briggs Cunningham. He intended to install the parts in his car, but never got around to it. "I remember Daddy used to drive me to school in the Cunningham," Leslie says.

After a few phone conversations, Schoendorf realized that he had discovered the only missing Cunningham C-3. But when he drove east across Connecticut to see the car, he was disappointed—the

As Sefried aged, he looked out the window of his home as the car slowly deteriorated. Look carefully and you can see that the front suspension collapsed because the crossmember had deteriorated.
TOM COTTER

car was in terrible condition after being parked outside for so long, even though the empty garage stood just 50 feet away. Rust had penetrated so severely that the chassis' front cross member had deteriorated, causing the front suspension to collapse. And even though the Italian-made Vignale body was made of aluminum, much of the body's steel substructure was severely cancerous.

Leslie declined Schoendorf's offer to buy it, saying she would rather restore it in memory of her father. Schoendorf suggested, though, that instead of opting for an expensive restoration, he would be glad to oversee a less expensive, sympathetic refurbishment.

Before the repairs began, the car was displayed in the Barn-Find class at the Fairfield County Concours d'Elegance in Connecticut. "The car won the best barn-find class," Schoendorf says, "and the crowd flipped!"

Since then, #5209 has been partially restored and displayed at a Cunningham Gathering at Lime Rock Park in Connecticut, where it won an award over several other, concours-winning C-3s.

Leslie likes to think that her father, Harry, was watching it all from the window of his new residence, somewhere up there.

CHAPTER 62
The Slime-Green Streamline Baby

In high school, Brian Barr drove the car everyone else wanted—a 1972 Datsun 240 Z. It wasn't just a white or beige 240 Z, typical of sports cars in those disco-days of 1978; no, Barr's car was lime green.

Growing up in western New York, Barr's Z-car saw lots of spirited back-road driving and trips to the nearby Watkins Glen racetrack. Unfortunately, the car also saw its share of wintertime snow and salt. So even though he attempted to modify the car—including a front air dam referred to as a "spook"—the salt gremlins were doing damage to the car's substructure.

Barr loved the Datsun, but college, career, marriage, and other cars—especially Porsches—took priority, so he eventually sold the rusty Z. It was gone, but not forgotten.

Decades later, with the desire to turn back the hands of time, he kept his eyes open for an original 240 Z. Coincidently, Barr, 52, heard of an early Z in his adopted hometown of Huntersville, North Carolina, and eventually tracked it down.

The story was intriguing.

The man selling the car had inherited it from his deceased sister-in-law's estate. In 1972, his sister-in-law and her husband went to their local Datsun dealership in Connecticut and each bought a new 240 Z; his was orange, and hers was lime green.

Things were going well for the sporty couple until she became ill in the late 1970s. Bedridden, her husband took her beloved Z off the road and parked

This is the 1972 Datsun 240Z that Brian Barr drove to high school when he got his driver's license at 16 years old. Rust and lifestyle changes forced him to part with the car a few years later. BRIAN BARR

it in the garage. Everyone had hoped her ailment was temporary and that she would soon be back on Connecticut roads in her brilliant Datsun, but that was not the case. When she passed away, the Datsun was forgotten for the next few decades, languishing in the garage.

Eventually, her husband decided to clean out the garage and asked his brother-in-law if he wanted the Datsun. He said yes, and that's how the car made its way to North Carolina, which is where his brother-in-law lived.

The brother-in-law drove the car for a while, but mostly used his pickup truck for business, so the 240 Z languished once more. Eventually, he parked the car in his front yard with a fat for-sale sign on the windshield.

It's all big hair, leisure suits, and white shoes for Barr again; he found a near replica of the 240Z he sold decades ago. The car is surprisingly solid and complete. BRIAN BARR

Barr almost went through the windshield of his truck when he spotted the car near his home. It was the same as his high school sports car—Lime Green paint, black interior, and stock hubcaps.

He had to have it.

After hearing the story, the previous owner heard Barr's offer and accepted it right there. Currently, Barr is going through the car, repairing small problems like rebuilding the carburetors and working through some electrical issues. Other than that, he's enjoying a rust-free replica of a car he enjoyed when life was simpler.

"When I saw this 51,000 mile example, I had to have it," he says. "It brings back great memories of my dad, mom, and my high school years. My thirty-fifth high school reunion is coming up, and I am driving the Z. Now if I could just find my leisure suit and platform shoes!"

CHAPTER 63

Hawaiian Hot Rod Party

S tan Kong graduated from McKinley High School in Honolulu, Hawaii, in 1960. In 1972, after a stint in the service, he left the island and moved to the Los Angeles area. He spent a career employed as a mechanic with American Airlines, and built hot rods and drag cars as a hobby. And a few years ago, he attended the McKinley 45th class reunion and was talking to some old classmates.

"We were talking about cars, and one of my class-mates said, 'My cousin is selling a '32 Ford roadster,'"

Kong says. "So after the reunion, I went over to see it. Luckily, the car had been covered with junk and the garage door was broken, so nobody knew it was in there."

According to Kong, the car was built, chopped, and channeled by Haruo Morishige in the 1950s, and featured in *Hot Rod* magazine in 1959. When the builder died, the car was left to his brother, who had no interest in it, so it sat for many years.

"It was dark when I got to the garage, and I couldn't really see it," he says. "One thing I did notice

Stan Kong followed up a lead while attending his 45th high school reunion in Honolulu and wound up owning this vintage 1932 Ford hot rod roadster.

JIM BARRETT

Kong brought the car back to his California home and restored it mechanically. The car, which had once been featured in *Hot Rod* magazine, is powered by a worked flathead V-8. JIM BARRETT

was that the car had been covered with a bed sheet, which over the years stuck to the car's lacquer paint."

Kong's classmate, who told him of the car, asked if he wanted to make an offer. "I told her, 'I really don't know what it looks like, but any '32 Ford roadster must be worth $10,000,'" he says.

She said she would think about it. She called Kong two weeks later, and they had a deal. By this time he was back in California, but he quickly returned to Hawaii to "unearth" his new purchase. He removed all the junk that had covered the car and pulled it from the garage. Then he dragged it to his friend's house nearby. Once the car was back in the sunlight after so many years, word quickly spread amongst the Hawaiian hot rod community.

"I can't believe I lost this '32 Ford right in my neighborhood," was a common comment from local gearheads. "How did some guy from the mainland buy it?" they wondered.

Kong shipped the car back to California, where he conducted a mechanical refurbishment. Even though he purchased the car with a small-block Chevy engine, the car was originally built with a Ford flathead V-8 and a 1939 Ford gearbox. So he built up a flathead with period speed equipment and installed it in the roadster.

It took about six months for Kong to go through the running gear as he corrected areas that were compromised when it was first built. "In Hawaii, it was hard to get the right parts in the 1950s, so, like the brake lines, they were copper," he said. "They needed to be changed to steel to be safe. I could have easily doubled my money on it if I wanted to sell it," he says.

But Kong is a hot rodder, not a dealer.

High School Hot Rod

More than four decades after graduating from Pindry High, Rob Gibby experienced a high school fantasy.

No, it wasn't finally dating that cheerleader he had a crush on, but for Gibby, it may have been an even more meaningful fantasy—he had found the actual Model A hot rod that he drove to Pindry High in 1959.

The romance with this certain Model A coupe began in 1956 when Gibby paid $50 for the bone-stock car on his 14th birthday. "My dad took me to a junkyard in New Jersey," the 70-year-old Gibby says. "They gave me a push start with a crane and it started right up. I drove it home from there."

His father also bought him a junkyard 265 cubic-inch Chevy, and the young Gibby was on his way to building his high school hot rod. He installed a '37 Buick gearbox and a '40 Ford rear end, and drove the car until he left for college in 1960, when he sold it for $300.

In 1987, he began looking for his old ride. A "want ad" turned up a red coupe that looked familiar. "I asked the owner a few questions and realized I found my old car!" Gibby says. Of course he had to buy it.

The car had been modernized over the years, but Gibby, along with pal Bob Outwater, returned the Model A to its 1950s specs. In 2010, Gibby drove his rebuilt hot rod to his 50th class reunion. It was an immediate hit with his classmates.

Gibby declined to say whether he drove home with one of the cheerleaders.

Rob Gibby (driving) purchased a stock Model A Ford for $50 on his 14th birthday in 1956. With the help of his dad and the local junkyard, he installed a Chevy engine and had the coolest hot rod in high school. ROB GIBBY

This is how Gibby's Model A looked when he repurchased it almost 40 years later. It was equipped with a modern drivetrain and air conditioning. Gibby is now rebuilding the car to the same condition as when he drove it to school in Perth Amboy, New Jersey. ROB GIBBY

CHAPTER 65
Better To Have Loved And Lost

Go ahead and criticize me now: I didn't buy the MG TC.

There is no good excuse, since I knew about the car since the mid-'60s, when I was 12 years old or so, when I would ride my bicycle in Lake Grove, Long Island, past the green MG. In the driveway was a man perpetually tinkering with it. I stopped and looked at the MG for a moment but was too young to pursue its purchase, so I got back on my bike and kept riding.

For years, as I passed the house while I lived on Long Island, I thought of that TC, a car that I had developed a passion for but unfortunately was never in a position to consider owning. Decades passed, and I moved to North Carolina to become involved in professional motorsports.

Years later, probably in the early 1990s, while my wife, Pat, our newborn son, Brian, and I were visiting my in-laws on Long Island, I got a little bit stir-crazy. I loaded Brian into his baby car seat and we went for a drive.

As I passed the Lake Grove home, I wondered, "Might that MG still be sitting in the garage?" I pulled over and peered into the garage door windows.

There it was!

Nearly 30 years after first seeing the car in the driveway, the car was still owned by the family. I carried Brian up to the house and rang the doorbell.

As a car-crazy kid on a bicycle, I remember seeing this MG TC in a garage back in the mid-1960s. Thirty years later, when I peeked in the same garage door, it was still there! TOM COTTER

Owner Nancy Sullivan of New York purchased the car in the 1950s and drove it on her honeymoon and on a number of trips to Watkins Glen for the U.S. Grand Prix. It had a few slight modifications, including cycle front fenders that steer with the front wheels. TOM COTTER

A woman answered. Her name was Nancy Sullivan. And the story she told me was incredible.

Nancy Moore purchased the slightly modified MG in 1957. Soon thereafter, she met another car enthusiast, Dennis Sullivan, who collected Model T Fords. Two years later, they were married, drove the MG to Cape Cod for their honeymoon, and then drove it up to the Canadian border.

Back on Long Island, the couple became caught up in the thriving sports car movement. They drove the little green car to races at Bridgehampton, Lime Rock, and Watkins Glen. When children started to arrive, the MG remained the family's favorite mode of transport. Dennis fabricated two baby seats in the package area behind the seat and regularly commuted to upstate New York to visit relatives.

In 1966, probably soon after I saw the car as a 12-year-old, the Sullivans sold the MG to a local enthusiast. Dennis died in 1975, and Nancy had an urge to regain the happy times she and Dennis shared. So when she saw her old MG for sale a few months afterward, she bought it back. The car sat for years in her garage, and she toyed with selling it.

She and I spoke about it that day in the early 1990s, but we couldn't decide on a price that was satisfactory for both of us. So I never pursued it.

But Tony Giordano, who read *The Cobra in the Barn*, asked if I minded if *he* pursued the purchase of the car.

"Go ahead, Tony," I said. "Have fun."

Well, he bought it, and he's having fun. Better to have loved and lost than never to have loved at all.

CHAPTER 66
College-Bound Franklin

Full disclosure: I recently accepted an invitation to join the advisory board at McPherson College, the Kansas college that specializes in teaching automotive restoration to students. And Jeff Stone, who contributed to this story, recently graduated from McPherson.

What does that mean? Really, just that both Jeff and I are total old car freaks.

This story begins long before Stone, 41, was enrolled at McPherson, back to when he was just eight years old. "A friend of my father's, Mark Palmer, bought this old car, a 1928 12 B Franklin," Stone says, who today works in the auto parts business. "He asked my dad to help him pull it out of the barn, so I went with him."

Stone inherited his love for old cars—Model T and Model A Fords—from his father. "My father was always into Model As, and his '64 Chevy pickup," he says. Old cars were a favorite Stone-family activity, so helping a friend retrieve an old car was the perfect way for the father and son to spend a Saturday.

Stone spent much of his youth accompanying his father on automotive excursions throughout the Midwest, resurrecting one car or another. "Apparently the owner of the Franklin had passed away," Stone says. "He had been a plumber, so we had to shift lots of plumbing materials before the car could be moved."

Buyer Mark Palmer confirms this. "It was buried in stuff," Palmer says, who first saw the car in 1976 but bought it in 1980. "It was buried up to its windows in

When he was just eight years old, Jeff Stone and his father helped family friend Mark Palmer move a 1928 Franklin out of a barn. This is what it looked like when it appeared at Palmer's home.
MARK PALMER

Deciding the barn-find Franklin required too much work, Palmer bought a second Franklin; this one. The original barn-find car was donated to McPherson College, where students are restoring it.
MARK PALMER

plumbing and heating junk." So father and son helped move the Franklin to Palmer's house. And that was the last Stone had seen or heard of that car for decades.

In his 30s, Stone had what he calls his "midlife crisis," and enrolled in McPherson College's auto restoration program. "Some people buy a Corvette, but I went to restoration school," he says. There, students learn hands-on fabrication, painting, mechanics, electrical systems, and upholstery. Additionally, students must learn automotive history and business.

Stone graduated McPherson with a Business degree in Automotive Restoration Management. While studying there, he often visited his parents' home in nearby Wichita. One day he mentioned to his father that he was working on an old four-door Franklin in the school's shop.

"I told my dad that we had replaced the structural wood in the body and repaired and test-fit new sheet metal," Stone says. Between Stone and his father, they surmised that the old sedan was actually the Franklin that they had extracted from a barn decades earlier. A call to Palmer confirmed their suspicion. "Mr. Palmer donated the car to the college in 1998," Stone says.

"Franklins are rare and hard to get parts for," Palmer adds. "Plus, I realized that I was not an auto restorer. The car deserved a proper restoration, so I donated it to the college."

And at the same time, a 1928 automobile was able to introduce the 41-year-old John Stone to his eight-year-old self.

CHAPTER 67

It Only Gets Better With Age

It's a typical story: two fraternity brothers in the mid-1960s shared a common interest of sports cars, so when they weren't involved in the other collegiate male activities—party going, beer drinking, girl ogling, and (of course) studying—they bought, wrenched, and drove sports cars.

That same story probably could have been written at any college in the United States during the heyday of the sports car. But for two frat brothers—Bob Pense and Frank Rotunda—the story played out again 50 years later.

Pense and Rotunda both grew up on Long Island, but met in 1964 when they were freshmen at Rutgers.

Fraternity brothers Bob Pense and Frank Rotunda dragged this $75 1957 Austin Healey 100-6 back to their dorm in 1964. They repaired and sold it soon thereafter. BOB PENSE

Eventually Pense's love for Austin Healeys rubbed off on Rotunda.

"He had a beautiful red 1958 that we drove between our homes and school," Rotunda says, who today lives in California. "Bob would find project cars in various states of disrepair, which led to many adventures."

One adventure was when a fellow Rutgers student was selling his blue 1957 100-6. The seller said the block was cracked and the clutch was shot. "He had planned to junk the car, but thought he might get lucky and sell it for a few bucks," Rotunda says. "So Bob took a chance and bought it for $75."

The friends hooked a tow bar to the Healey's front bumper and began their 60-mile trek home. Since the car didn't track well, Rotunda "volunteered" to sit behind the wheel and steer as needed. When they crested an Interstate exit ramp, the bumper bolts broke off and the Healey was free-wheeling!

"In a rush of adrenaline," he says, "I found the brake pedals, hoping they'd work," he says.

They did, and the Healey came to a halt. The two had a good laugh (and probably more than a few beers) when it was all said and done. But first they had to get it home—they were still about five miles from Pense's house, and towing was no longer an option.

"What to do?" Rotunda wondered. "Bob had a little gas in his trunk, so we thought we might just see if the motor might fire up. He jumped in, pumped the weak clutch pedal, I gave it a push down the ramp and—bump, bump, bump—off he goes."

The car reappeared on Craigslist 44 years later. They oiled down the cylinders, installed new points and plugs, and it fired right up!
BOB PENSE

Rotunda jumped in the tow car and gave chase. It turns out the "cracked block" was actually a popped freeze-out plug, and the "shot" clutch only needed a cylinder rebuild. So for the cost of $5, the Healey was returned to running condition.

Pense and Rotunda cleaned up the car and sold it for $525. They didn't think much about it until 44 years later when John Moore, one of Pense's friends, saw an old blue Healey with white racing stripes on Craigslist.

When he showed Pense the listing, Pense was incredulous. "*That's* my car?"

The Healey was still on Long Island, not far from where he sold it decades earlier. Moore bought the car, and he and Pense soaked down the cylinders with WD-40, installed new fuel, points, and plugs, and it started right up! To this day, Pense is helping his friend get the numbers-matching car road-worthy again.

Note: A version of this story first appeared in the November 2013 issue of the Antique Automobile Club of America's (AACA) Speedster *magazine.*

CHAPTER 68

Check Out The Block On This One

As a young guy in the 1960s, what could be cooler than to own a big-block Chevy? Nuttin!

So in February 1969—when Chick Renn of York, Pennsylvania, was 20 years old—he went down to Ammon R. Smith Chevrolet in his town and, with just $25, ordered a brand new, dark green 1969 Nova, complete with a 375-horsepower 396 L78 engine, Turbo-hydramatic, bucket seats, console, gauges, the works.

The only problem was that he had to wait until he turned 21 to apply for the loan.

On April 17, 1969, one week after his 21st birthday, he signed the loan papers and drove the car home. Recently married, his wife, Karen, drove the hot Nova back and forth to work for a couple of years. Then, in 1972, Renn took the Nova off the road for the occasional drag race. "I never wanted to hack up the metal, so I never installed a roll bar," Renn says, now 65. "I only modified the torque converter, added headers and slicks, things like that." Then, the car sat. And sat.

In 1983, with just 24,700 miles on the odometer, Renn sold his beloved Nova to a man in Poughkeepsie, New York. That man sold it to a man in Massachusetts who sold it to a man in Pennsylvania, who sold it to a man in Ohio.

In 2011, Renn got a call from a friend who was attending the GM Nationals at Carlisle, Pennsylvania. "Hey, Chick," his friend Skip Lecatas (who you read

Chick Renn bought this 396 Nova new in 1969, drove it on the street, and did some drag racing. Here it is coming off the line at York US 30 Raceway, making a pass of 11.97 seconds at 115.68 mph. CHICK RENN

about in the Yenko Nova story in chapter 35) says, "I just met the guy who owns your old Nova!"

Lecatas gave the owner Renn's phone number, and the man promised to call because he wanted some old photographs of the Nova for his show display. One year later, the man finally decided to call Renn. "Hey, I'm going to display your old car at the GM Nationals this year," the owner said. "Why don't you come down and take a look?"

So Renn drove to Carlisle.

"It's 2012, and it's the first time I've seen my old Nova in over 29 years," Renn says. The two men

Renn sold the car with only 24,700 miles on it in 1983. In 2013, 30 years after selling it, he purchased his Nova back with only 31,849 miles. CHICK RENN

talked for a couple of hours, and as he was leaving, Renn turned to the man and said, "If you ever decide to sell, let me know."

One year later, in June 2013, again at the GM Nationals, the two men talked again, striking a deal for the Nova. "I bought my old car back," Renn says. "After selling it 30 years ago with 24,700 miles, when I bought it back, it only had 31,849 miles.

"Even got back my old 1972 license plate that was on the car when originally sold and all my old paperwork," he adds, "including my old title, owner's card, Ammon R. Smith order form, and bill of sale, warranty, P.O.P, and 1973 registration sticker.

"The car's in great shape and still has the original paint, engine, and drivetrain. We're just going to drive and enjoy it. This time," Renn notes with relief, "it's staying in the family."

CHAPTER 69

A Woman's Intuition
(Grand Prix Premonition)

by Mark Henderson

Perhaps this story is about a journey as much as a rediscovery. It begins in early 1969, when my brother Dave Henderson ordered a new Pontiac Grand Prix SJ from Skeie Motors in Ames, Iowa. Completely redesigned for 1969, the Grand Prix was John DeLorean's statement to the automotive world of what a personal luxury muscle car should be. This stunning example in Castilian Bronze featured a 428 cubic-inch 370 horsepower motor, a rare Muncie four-speed option, and a Safe-T-Track differential, along with an AM-FM radio, air conditioning, and automatic level control.

The car served as Dave's regular transportation for nearly nine years until he sold it to me in January 1978. I was thrilled and proud to bring the Grand Prix home to Dayton, Ohio, where it became my own daily driver. The GP was also pressed into service for important life events, such as limousine duty when my wife and I were married that September and when our two new baby daughters came home from the hospital over the following years.

In September 1981, the Grand Prix was severely damaged during an errand run while preparing for a family move. A fuel line leak caused an underhood fire that spread into the interior. Unfortunately, with new job responsibilities and a young family, I had to let the GP go.

Accepting a meager insurance settlement, I sold the car's remains to Bob Morris in Dayton. He masterfully completed a frame-off restoration over the next two years. I generally lost track of the car over time, although Bob occasionally kept in contact to share stories of interest.

In August 2004, my wife "got the feeling" that we should look for our old car and see if we could buy it back. Approaching Bob Morris first, he reported he had sold the GP in 1994 but couldn't remember the buyer's name. With help from an Internet group that

Our 1969 Grand Prix SJ was a daily driver that included plenty of winter use in the Ohio region. This photo shows the car buried in the driveway by the Blizzard of 1978. MARK HENDERSON

Today the Grand Prix enjoys much easier duty, but is still driven and enjoyed quite frequently. MARK HENDERSON

specializes in 1969–72 Grands Prix, we eventually discovered a car very similar to ours that was sold at Barrett-Jackson in January 1999. B-J's documentation included a VIN, and Bob's records confirmed that the numbers matched those from our old car. Using savvy advice from a great friend, we approached Barrett-Jackson's management to request they pass our information along to the buyers should they ever decide to sell. Miraculously, Steve and Cindy Wade in Washington State already had the car advertised for sale. All the numbers still matched, colors were as original, and the car had been very well maintained

by both the Wades and another previous owner, Tom Kelley. We made a deal, and just before Christmas 2004, the GP arrived home in Kokomo, Indiana.

With no real information to begin from and after a 23-year absence, we were humbly blessed that our old Grand Prix found its way back to us after just four months of searching. The GP rejoined our family in time to transport both of our daughters to their individual weddings, and to eventually bring our first granddaughter home in style. Our thanks go out to the GP's past caretakers across seven states for their care of the car, and also for their friendship today.

XI

TALK THE TALK, WALK THE WALK

CHAPTER 70
Hot Gossip

One lesson Adam White learned from reading *Cobra in the Barn* is that if you hope to discover a great barn find, you need to talk about cars to everyone you meet. Period. Take it from big-time barn-finder Jay Leno—he suggests talking cars with mechanics, postmen, landscapers, and police officers.

Well, White recently applied that lesson, and it paid off in spades.

White was riding in a truck helping to deliver a copy machine near Charlotte, North Carolina, when the conversation with the driver turned to old cars. White lamented how his perennial favorites are classic Jaguars. What the driver said next was the most intriguing kind of news White could have hoped for:

"I know someone who has a bunch of old Jaguars."

White's obsession with Jags goes back to when he was a teenager growing up on Long Island, New York, in the 1970s. One of his first jobs in high school was at a repair shop for imported cars. "Even Jaguar engines are elegant," White says.

"So I finally met the truck driver's friend, Franziska Long, and her father, Graham, and saw their amazing collection in their backyard and barn. The barn was packed with six Jags, a couple of parts cars, and loads of parts and shop equipment," he says. "There were a pair of XK-120 Roadsters, a pair of XK-150 Coupes, an early E-Type Coupe, and a MK I sedan, which looked like a wedding car." The cars had been stored

By mentioning to a stranger that he liked old Jaguars, Adam White was turned onto the Jaguar discovery of a lifetime. Graham Long acquired a dozen Jags over the years, all stored in this cramped barn. TOM COTTER

and forgotten for a long time. White wanted to find out how they all arrived there.

He discovered that Graham had been quite an adventurer in his youth. Now 70, Graham suffers

Long drove this XK120 across Australia, Africa, and Europe as a young man. The collection includes coupes, sedans, and another roadster.
TOM COTTER

from dementia. But as a young man, he drove one of the XK-120 Roadsters, a 1951, across Australia, the length of Africa, and across Europe before arriving back home in England. After moving to Charlotte with his Jaguar in 1982, Graham began buying additional Jaguars and parts.

"He bought Jags and parts cars from Pennsylvania, New York, and Alabama," White says. "He also scoured junkyards throughout the East Coast, acquiring numerous engines, gearboxes, and other parts."

White discovered that Graham was quite a mechanic; he converted the MK I sedan to MK IV disc brakes and Weber Carburetors. "And he didn't like 4.2-liter engines, so he converted the E-type to

an earlier 3.8-liter engine, complete with Carrillo connecting rods and Weber carbs," White says. "It's a valuable engine."

Lately, the family has been faced with a dilemma; since their father is no longer able to maintain the cars, his children are considering selling the collection. "He has two sons, one of whom lives in England, and each is interested in a Jag," White says. "And Franziska would like to sell the rest of the cars to help finance her father's care."

Franziska asked White, the ultimate Jaguar enthusiast, whether he'd like to own one of the projects.

"If I had the cash, I'd love to own any one of those cars," he says. "Just not right now."

CHAPTER 71
Alfa-Bet Soup For The Soul

"We were lucky."

That is how professional barn-finder Daniel Rapley sums up a nice stash of unusual cars he recently stumbled upon. Rapley hunts for cars for a living, so his ears are always tuned for leads. He readily admits that he may have the perfect career.

"I got a call from a friend who told me about a vintage Alfa Romeo Giulietta that was sitting in Salina, Kansas," Rapley, a Brit who lives in Connecticut, says. "I kept calling the guy for a year."

When Rapley finally connected with the car's owner, the man revealed that, no, he didn't have just one Alfa—he actually had *seven* Alfas and a small

Seeing a scene like this is enough to make any sports car enthusiast's heart beat faster. Daniel Rapley had a challenge figuring out which parts went to which cars! DANIEL RAPLEY

warehouse filled with Alfa parts. For an Alfista, that is also known as Heaven.

"The man had lost his lease on his warehouse, so he needed to sell all the cars and parts," Rapley says. "I decided to make him an offer on the entire collection."

The man accepted the offer. The hard work was about to begin. "His warehouse was so packed, we could hardly move," Rapley says. "All seven cars were disassembled, and those parts were mixed up with all the other parts."

"It was quite an event," Rapley adds. "We rented an 18-wheeler, a fork lift, and a 26-foot box truck. On the way back to Connecticut, the truck broke down twice, and the truck driver was only arrested once." (Unfortunately for readers, Rapley didn't provide any details to the arrest.)

Despite those challenges, the load finally arrived at Rapley's shop in Connecticut. It was then, during the unloading process, that he was finally able to inspect his new purchase. One car in particular intrigued Rapley: a matching-numbers 1956 Alfa 1900.

The rare Alfa Romeo 1900 sports sedan was designed by Orazio Satta for the Alfa Romeo company in 1950. It was Alfa's first car built entirely on a production line. It was also Alfa's first production car without a separate chassis. The model was introduced for the first time in 1950 at the Paris Motor Show.

"It had been sitting in the Arizona desert," he says of the nearly six-decade-old, yet solid car. "It was only missing some glass and a seat."

Buying these cars was one challenge; having them shipped from the Midwest to Connecticut—when some didn't have suspensions—was another. DANIEL RAPLEY

Besides the 1900, the hoard included: a 1955 Giulietta Sprint (which Rapley said could be the oldest in the United States); a 1957 Sprint; two 1958 Spider Veloces; 1959 Spider Normale; and a 1967 Giulia Spider.

Rapley has spent the past few months picking through his piles of parts and slowly putting his cars back together. "I've sold a couple of the cars to people in the Northeast, where lots of folks are knowledgeable about Alfas," he says. "Fortunately they were able to help me decide which parts were correct for each car."

Surrounded by the constant flow of cool cars that come and go through his doors, what kind of car does professional barn-finder Rapley drive himself?

"Well, at home I drive a Toyota," he says. "Or whatever car I rent at the airport when I'm looking for more cars." Not a bad way to live.

CHAPTER 72
Back Door Barn-Find Access

In my previous barn-find books, I've listed careers that are ideal for barn-finders—landscapers, policemen, and delivery people, for example. The reason? These people can legally enter private property and potentially see what is invisible from the street.

But Alan Szarek may have the very best career for barn-finding: he's a certified auto appraiser! Szarek is called by folks who desire to sell their cars. That includes cars that have been hibernating in garages for decades.

We should all be jealous.

Recently, Szarek received a call to appraise what was called a 1946 Cisitalia Pininfarina Custom. The Italian Cisitalia brand was one of the first post–World War II manufacturers to take aerodynamics seriously. The sleek bodywork was a good match for the small Fiat 1,100 and 1,500 engines. Cisitalia pushed automotive design forward; perhaps that's why one sits as part of the permanent collection at New York's Museum of Modern Art.

The Cisitalia Szarek inspected had been sitting in the garage of his client's father-in-law for decades. And it had been modified. The "Custom" in the car's name means that the 1,500 cc Fiat engine had been removed a long time ago and replaced with a small-block Chevy, apparently in 1955.

Further modifications included an Oldsmobile rear and a Heidt's front suspension, meaning that this would be a difficult car to source original parts for a

If this barn-find Cisitalia had been left unmodified, it could have been worth a small fortune in restored condition. Unfortunately, it had been converted long ago to a Ford V-8, so many original were parts were lost. DAVID WILLIAMS

concours restoration. Surprisingly, though, the car in its current condition—even though very rough and modified—is still quite valuable. Cisitalia 202 models like this one are rare and in demand, so even though the investment to correctly restore this car would be steep, Szarek's appraisal was $86,900.

So it's not priceless, but for the average consumer, it's close enough. And you can't put a price on beauty.

CHAPTER 73

Going Down South

When one thinks of Savannah, Georgia, thoughts of historic buildings, seafood cafes, and a beautiful waterfront often come to mind.

Certainly not old sports cars.

But master car hunter Ernie Cabrera, who actually lives four hours away in Atlanta, has scored some terrific automotive discoveries in that seaside town. The semi-retired real estate investor has owned some very desirable sports cars in the past 45 years, including a Porsche 550 Spyder and a 1953 Porsche Cabriolet.

Cabrera's first "Savannah find" was the 1958 Porsche 356 A Cabriolet he discovered in the 1970s. The car was a European delivery and went to Oregon before landing in Savannah. "I traded my 1961 sunroof coupe for the cabriolet," Cabrera says. "The car had no rust, so I took it to a body shop to be restored."

When it reappeared from the shop three years later, the body was cherry, but Cabrera had lost interest in the car. So he parked the disassembled convertible in his own garage, where it has sat for the past 40 years. He is only now beginning to complete that restoration.

And in 2003, Savannah yielded a second Porsche to Cabrera. "It was a 1957 Porsche Speedster," he says. "The owner had died and his daughter was selling her dad's assets in an estate sale."

A friend of Cabrera's, who was a member of the Porsche Club of America, had been contacted by the daughter, asking him how she might sell a car like

Ernie Cabrera has had terrific luck with finding cool cars in just one city: Savannah, Georgia. He traded a Porsche 356 sunroof coupe for this Cabriolet back in the 1970s and still owns it today. ERNIE CABRERA

this. That friend called Cabrera and they struck a deal. "The car had been sitting since at least 1990," he says. "It was partially disassembled."

"In those days, fiberglass was the hero, so at some point, the car had fiberglass cloth applied over the entire floor. So moisture was captured under that and it rusted badly."

But other than that, Cabrera says the car was fairly complete and cleaned up pretty well. "I just changed the oil, cleaned the carbs, flushed the gas tank, and it ran fine." This Speedster was sold to a collector in Europe in 2008.

Cabrera's third Savannah discovery was the 1961 Alfa Giulietta he bought in 2013. The same friend that told him about the '57 Speedster told him about the Alfa. "The car had been sitting for a good 30 years in a barn," he says. "The owner was too sick to work on it."

This car also had fiberglass slathered all over the floors, but in this case, Cabrera credits it for actually having saved the Alfa's floors. At some point the owner attempted to do a brake job, but got ill and couldn't finish it. So Cabrera is still missing the brake shoes and return springs. "But when I put some gas in the carburetor float bowls, the car started right up and idled perfectly," he says.

"The paint isn't shiny, but it looks pretty good. Fortunately the car was never modified, so it's still all original. I'm going to just leave it as-is and drive it."

And if it should break, well, he knows where to find another.

Cabrera is particularly excited about this 1958 Alfa Giulietta he found in, you guessed it, Savannah. He has owned dozens of cool barn-find cars throughout the years. ERNIE CABRERA

CHAPTER 74
Should Have Made It A Threesome

Between 1970 and 1972, Steve McCain heard of two very neglected 1955 Corvettes: one he bought, and the other he sincerely regrets not buying.

McCain was still in high school, already in love with early Corvettes during a time when the rest of us were in love with the late model versions. "Back then, everyone who owned a Corvette automatically got a subscription to *Corvette News*," McCain says. "In one of those issues, they did a search for the oldest 1953 Corvette in existence. I thought the car looked really neat, and decided I wanted one."

McCain, who lives in Summerfield, North Carolina, heard about a 1955 Corvette sitting behind a house in nearby Lexington, about an hour away. "It

It took McCain four years to restore the Corvette. The early fiberglass work—rough even from the factory—had begun to deteriorate from sitting in the elements. STEVE MCCAIN

was parked in the backyard of the owner's parents," he says. "It was in pretty sad shape."

McCain wanted to check the VIN tag, which he was told was mounted on the steering column, but the tag wasn't there. "The owner didn't know where it was either," he says.

But McCain finally found the tag on the driver's side doorjamb. The VIN # read #VE55S001001, which translates to:

V = V-8
E = Corvette Series
55 = Model Year
S = St. Louis Assembly Plant, where the car was produced
001 = All 1953–1955 Corvettes had this designation
001 = The very first 1955 Corvette off the production line

McCain had scored! For a negotiated price of $500, he bought the very first 1955 Corvette to roll off the assembly line. Not bad, even in 1970.

Two years later, he heard about another 1955 Corvette in a Wilkesboro, North Carolina, junkyard for $1,000. He had to investigate. "It was also in pretty sad shape," McCain says. "And it had this big headrest molded into the trunk, holes drilled in the frame, and holes where a small windscreen had mounted.

Steve McCain followed up a lead on a 1955 Corvette, one of seven hundred built, which was near Lexington, North Carolina. The car was in pretty sad condition, but at the $500 asking price, he feels he got a pretty good deal. STEVE MCCAIN

"It was a botched up car for $1,000, and I didn't need another '55 anyway. So I didn't buy it."

It was only later that he heard that Smokey Yunick had four 1955 Corvettes with headrests molded into the trunks and that the one in the Wilkesboro junkyard was one of Smokey's. It had been used exclusively for testing at GM's Arizona test track.

He regrets not buying the car to this day, more than 40 years later. Nonetheless, he still had the #1 1955 Corvette he had purchased for $500, which he restored and sold in 1976 for $10,000 to a collector who also owned the first 1956 and first 1957 Corvettes built as well.

Since then, McCain has owned numerous Corvettes, including one 1953, four 1954s, and one 1955. But does he regret selling 1955 #1?

"If I still owned the car today, I think it would be more historically significant than the last 1967 big-block, which bid to $600,000 at the 2007 Barrett-Jackson auction, but it wouldn't necessarily be more valuable. These older cars are just not as popular as the later ones."

Not to most people, at least. To McCain, they're everything.

CHAPTER 75
She Wore Nightmist

Al Puhalla had just bought a 1968 Shelby GT500 and mentioned it to his banker.

"Did you buy the one in Lewiston?" the banker asked.

The banker had just returned from a function and heard of a guy who had died. His sister was selling the estate, and part of that estate included a 1967 GT350 that had been on blocks, partly disassembled in the basement since 1985.

She wouldn't take less than $80,000.

"This guy started to buy parts to restore the car in 1986," says Puhalla, 59, from Clarence, Pennsylvania. "There were loads of NOS parts in an upstairs bedroom, including decals, trim, rubber, taillights, bumpers, and various hardware."

Puhalla concluded that the Shelby was an LA Airport car, which means it was built at Shelby's facility near LAX. It was originally Nightmist Blue metallic with white stripes. The 94,000-mile, "close-headlight" car came from the factory with a four-speed gearbox, AM radio, and power steering.

He made an offer of $80,000, and by the following Wednesday, the car was his.

When Puhalla went over to pick up the car, the sister had a few surprises for him, including the

This 1967 Shelby GT350 is known as an LA Airport car—one built at Shelby's facility near LAX airport.

original bill of sale, bank book, and a Shelby jacket her brother had purchased decades earlier.

The car had some rust, but no cancer. Nevertheless, he sandblasted the car for a full restoration.

"I've got the car and parts spread across about 2,000 square feet in my building," he says.

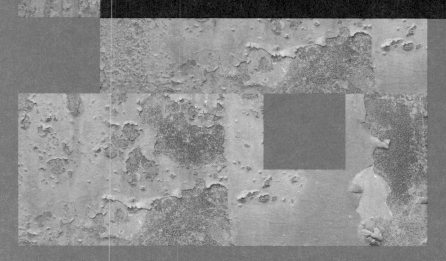

XII

SHE'S HAD SOME WORK DONE

CHAPTER 76

The Joy Of Six

The ad jumped out from a copy of *Hemmings Motor News* in 2000 to Joe Trybulec: 1954 Corvette, 15,000 miles, one owner, fuel-injected V-8 engine.

Apparently he was the only one who noticed it.

"Nobody paid attention to the ad because it was listed with a fuel-injected V-8," Trybulec of Bentonville, Arkansas, says. Corvette collectors stayed away in droves because they believed the six-cylinder sports car was a cobbled-up V-8 hot rod. But Trybulec pursued the car and discovered an incredible story.

The original six-cylinder engine had been removed in 1957 and replaced with a special fuel-injected

Joe Trybulec was the only one who called about this hybrid '54 Vette. It was listed as having a fuel injected V-8; '54s only came with six-cylinder engines. This one was last on the road in 1967. JOE TRYBULEC

The fuel-injected engine was actually a transplant from a 1957 Corvette that raced at Sebring. Trybulec had stumbled upon Corvette gold! JOE TRYBULEC

"Black Widow" 283 cubic-inch engine, which had actually powered a factory entry in that year's Sebring 12-Hour race.

The engine was originally in the factory-racing 1957 Corvette owned and raced by Ebb Rose of Houston, Texas. Rose's father owned Rose Trucking, which, in 1957, had purchased a large volume of new Chevy trucks for their business.

"After attending a dinner in Houston in appreciation for the Rose Trucking purchase of 100 trucks, GM President Ed Cole asked Rose to drive the new Corvette race cars in SCCA," Trybulec says. "After the 1957 AMA ban (which forbade American auto manufacturers from racing involvement), Cole sold Rose three Sebring Corvettes for $1 each."

Soon after the Corvette purchase, Rose was badly hurt when he crashed one of the Corvettes in a Louisiana road race. The car was shipped back to Rose's ranch in Texas for storage. "After crashing one of the production body Sebring Corvettes, the wrecked racecar was given to friend and mechanic George Moore with plans of transplanting the drivetrain into his '54 Corvette," Trybulec says.

Rose is reported to have told Moore to take the wrecked Corvette, because "I only paid one dollar for it."

Moore removed his Corvette's six-cylinder engine and replaced it with the Black Widow V-8, gearbox, and differential. He used the car on the road, but when his son was involved in an accident while driving the car, Moore put the car into his garage for a 30-year hibernation.

Trybulec followed up on the *Hemmings* ad. When he flew to Texas, checked out the car, and heard the story, he bought the car immediately from the Moore family.

Trybulec's friend, Ken Kayser—a long-time engineer at a GM engine plant—was able to confirm that the drivetrain actually had Sebring history. "That Sebring drivetrain was removed undisturbed, unrestored, and complete in 2007. It was displayed at the Bloomington Gold Special Collection 50th anniversary of the 1957 Corvette, Fuel Injection, and the T10 four-speed," Trybulec says.

"That unrestored Sebring engine is planned to return to the surviving Sebring car," he says. "So the 1954 Corvette continues to sit in my garage with only 15,000 miles on the odometer."

CHAPTER 77

Benny's Coupe

by Mark Henderson

The town of Connersville, Indiana, was home to a local industrialist named Ben Johnson. Johnson had an enviable collection of classic American and European automobiles during the 1950s and 1960s. His son Benny grew up enjoying cars as well but had more of a penchant for speed. Benny could buy nearly any hot rod he wanted, but in 1955, he decided to build one himself.

Benny began with a basic 1935 Ford coupe. His father had connections at GM, and he ordered a brand new 365 cubic-inch Cadillac El Dorado engine for the project. He eventually added a Latham supercharger with four YH-series side-draft carbs, and then he found a Ford top-loader gearbox to transfer power back into a Halibrand rear end. The four corners were outfitted with Ford solid steel rims and whitewall tires: 6.70"x15" in front, 8.20"x15" in

Benny Johnson's modified 1935 Ford coupe was renewed after its 36-year nap in a Connersville, Indiana barn. MARK HENDERSON

The 1956 Caddy El Dorado motor was built up with a Latham supercharger and four YH-series side-draft carbs. MARK HENDERSON

back. Hydraulic drum brakes all around assisted with high-speed stops.

The body was meticulously chopped, channeled, and sculpted. A louvered hood incorporated special cutouts for the carbs. The grille was sectioned, 1950 Buick headlights were integrated into the pontoon front fenders, and the running boards were removed. The cowl vent and rumble seat were smoothed in with lead. Custom gold and black gave the appearance of European refinement.

Interior details were well considered. Indy-style racing seats—rolled and pleated in black leather—had their outside bolsters modified for easy entry and exit. A custom Plexiglas headliner insert let the sun, moon, and stars shine inside. Stewart Warner gauges conveyed critical data to the driver.

Benny completed the coupe in 1956. He drove it until 1960, then he parked the car in his barn, where it sat for the next 36 years. Jim Robinson was a family friend and would occasionally express an interest in the coupe, but Benny never seemed inclined to sell. One day in 1996, Jim got the surprise of his life. He had completed some bodywork and paint on a car for Benny, and Benny simply *gave him the coupe as payment* so long as Jim agreed to repaint one more car in return. Of course, Jim accepted the deal and brought his prize home.

The coupe proved surprisingly easy to get back into running form. Jim began with a systematic cleaning inside and out then evaluated the mechanicals. The engine's internals required some minor attention and cleanup, but beyond that, only routine maintenance issues had to be dealt with. Jim and his wife, Lea Ann, continue to enjoy the coupe, frequently driving it to shows and on tours. They happily redirect any compliments back to Benny for his exquisite vision and craftsmanship.

CHAPTER 78

One Bitchin' Jag

Words like *bitchin'* are seldom used when discussing Jaguars. You might say *bitchin'* to describe, say, a '32 Ford HiBoy roadster or possibly a chopped 1949 Mercury coupe. But this Jaguar may have more in common with those cars than any of those Jags that participate at Concours d'Elegance or on road race circuits.

This Jag was built in 1935, so it was actually not even called a Jaguar yet. Instead, it was called an SS1 Tourer. The name SS, which stood for Swallow Sidecar, was dropped because Hitler referred to his secret police force as the SS, which stood for *Schutzstaffel*. The British automobile manufacturer wanted to distance itself from the conflicts across the English Channel, so in 1945, the name was changed to Jaguar.

So this SS1, or Jaguar, took a different route when it came to the United States than most others.

Before it was a Jaguar, this old bird was known as an SS1 Tourer.

The former owner swapped the engine, installing a Chrysler six-cylinder engine in place of the original 2.4-liter, flathead six-cylinder.

The SS1 was purchased by an American in the United Kingdom in 1948 or 1949 and brought to the States. The man's mechanic told him, "One day you're going to blow that engine and we won't be able to fix it." So when a rod went through the engine block, hot rod modifications began.

In 1950, when the car was 15 years old, the convertible top and windshield were chopped 2 inches. Then, the car was brought to the Carson Top Shop in Los Angeles, where one of their famous padded, upholstered, removable tops was installed. For a foreign car, especially an elegant model like the SS1, this was highly unusual. Later, the owner installed huge 10-inch P-100 headlights from a Rolls Royce.

The modifications continued under the hood, where he installed a modified Chrysler six-cylinder engine in place of the original 2.4-liter, flathead six-cylinder. "The Chrysler engine conversion looked like the original powerplant," says Hector Castro, owner of the car and proprietor of HRC Jaguars, a restoration shop in Denver, North Carolina. The new engine was adapted to the car's original four-speed gearbox. "The Chrysler engine was modified with triple carburetors on a custom manifold, high-compression pistons, high-lift camshaft and hand-made headers," he says.

The original SS rear end was utilized, but a Ford center section was adapted with a 3.60:1 ratio. "A friend of mine found the car, which had been sitting in Washington, for 25 years, and asked if I was interested in the car," Castro says.

The car still features its 1952 registration sticker on the back window. The interior—the four bucket seats and door panels—is also original.

Castro is in a bit of a quandary; his business specializes in restoring vintage Jaguars. But this car is special, especially since it was modified back in the day. "If I put the original engine back in, the car will never run as well as it does with the Chrysler," he says.

His current plan is to clean it up and enjoy the car as-is, with its dark blue paint and interior showing wonder patina (at least until he is able to secure all the original parts he needs to return it to original). That could take a while because the parts are extremely rare. Anybody got an old SS lying around?

CHAPTER 79

That Special Frick Touch

Bill Frick figures prominently into 1950s midget and sports car racing—and also into hot rod engine conversions. Frick raced and built some of the fastest midget racecars of the day, driven to many wins by a man named Ted Tappet, whose real name was Phil Walters. Later, Frick built many of the cars that sportsman Briggs Cunningham raced both in the United States and at LeMans.

But it was his engine conversions that are the subject of this story. Frick produced powerful hot rods called Fordillacs and Studillacs in his Long Island

shop—they were early 1950s Ford and Studebaker hybrids married with powerful Cadillac engines.

Tampa-based Frick historian Mark Elliott has been intrigued with Bill Frick for decades and hopes to write a book about the man. He once owned a very special 1949 Fordillac convertible and always stays on the lookout for Frick-built cars.

Recently, Elliott came across another Frick conversion that spurred his interest. A woman called him one day and said her deceased father-in-law had left her a 1957 Ford Thunderbird. Under the hood, the car featured a 389 cubic-inch Pontiac engine.

Looking like a restored 1957 Thunderbird, this car, still wearing its factory hubcaps, fooled many a street racer. The car was heavily modified by early hot rodder Bill Frick, whose shop on Long Island became famous for building 1950 Fordillacs.
ROLAND CASSIDY

"Who was Bill Frick and what is the car worth?" she asked.

Elliott offered to come to New Hampshire, where she lived, to inspect the car, but she consigned the car to a dealership before that trip could be arranged. "She had all the paperwork," Elliott says. "Her father-in-law was one of two brothers who owned an Esso gas station in Lowell, Massachusetts. Prior to the T-Bird, the brothers had owned other Bill Frick conversions: two Fordillacs and one Studillac. They bought the T-bird new and street-raced it for money.

Elliot learned that they first installed a supercharger and eventually even a second supercharger. "When that wasn't fast enough," he adds, "in 1959, Frick installed the Pontiac engine and two four-barrel carburetors."

The Pontiac's engine proved too powerful for the stock drivetrain, though, because the car was brought to Frick's shop on Long Island several times to repair a bent driveshaft. And from the documentation, Elliott discovered that Frick finally cured that recurring problem by installing a Ford ambulance driveshaft and rear end, which he felt were the most durable.

Even though Elliott collects interesting cars, they are usually of the sports car variety. "I didn't really need an old drag car," he says. The consigned dealer couldn't sell the car during the three-month contracted period, so the car was still available.

It was an intriguing find. Elliott obtained the original Frick build sheet and invoice. Even though the car looked bone-stock, right down to the hubcaps, it was very modified. The 389 Pontiac engine was over-bored by .030 inch.

"It had an overdrive transmission, which functionally made it a four-speed," Elliott says. "For traction, the brothers had an extra-long Continental kit installed, and filled the spare tire with concrete. Back in the day, I'm told the car could lift its front wheels

Things get suspicious in the back; that Continental Kit is about the longest we›ve ever seen. Rumor has it that the spare tire was filled with concrete to help with traction, and the long bumper acted as a wheelie bar. ROLAND CASSIDY

This engine compartment once contained a Ford 312 cubic-inch V-8, first with one supercharger, then two. The Ford powerplant was ditched, courtesy of Bill Frick, in favor of a big-block Pontiac engine, complete with two four barrel carburetors. ROLAND CASSIDY

off the ground 12 inches, so I guess the Continental kit served as a wheelie bar, too."

At last report, Elliott was trying to find a worthy home for this fascinating T-Bird. Interested?

XIII

OLDIES BUT BEAUTIES

CHAPTER 80

The AC Next Door

Because I've been searching for old cars since I was 14 years old, you might think I'd have searched every nook and cranny in my hometown of Davidson, North Carolina, for vintage tin. Actually, I've done a pretty good job of discovering the few cars within the town limits, but to my chagrin, one actually appeared right under my nose.

It was practically next door, literally. It was hidden my neighbor's barn!

It happened soon after my friend, *Road & Track* Editor-at-Large Peter Egan and I arrived at my home after the 3,300-mile cross-country commute of driving my 1965 Cobra from the San Francisco area to North Carolina (those were nine incredible days).

Soon after the story appeared in the January 2002 issue of *Road & Track*, I received a call from my neighbor, Hugh Barger. I had never met Barger, because his home was more than a half-mile from my house. "I just read about your A.C. Cobra, and wondered if I could take a look at it," he says. "We seem to have something in common."

I drove my Cobra to his house the following Saturday morning and visited with him and his lovely wife, Brenda, as they looked at my Cobra. Then he invited me into his barn.

When I was invited into Hugh Barger's barn, just one-half mile from my home, this is what I found. It is a 1962 AC Greyhound, and it was built on the same assembly line in England as my Cobra.
TOM COTTER

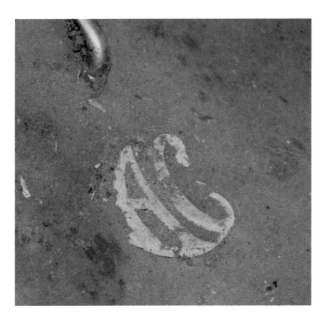

The car has been sitting for decades and has slowly sunk into the dirt floor, now resting on the chassis. Rats and raccoons appear to make the AC a super-highway. TOM COTTER

Now, I had driven past this barn for almost 20 years and was always curious if something interesting might lurk within. But I've so often been disappointed when searching through farmers' barns—most of the time, it's just a pile of hay. Or a Massey Ferguson.

Thankfully, I was wrong.

This barn, one-half mile from my house, contained an A.C. Greyhound, an aluminum four-seater coupe that had rolled off the same obscure assembly line in Thames Ditton, England, as my Cobra had a few years later.

Barger explained: "In the 1960s, my father sold my Alvis and bought me this A.C. Greyhound to drive to graduate school. Brenda and I used it for years when we lived near Washington, D.C. But when we moved back to Davidson, it wasn't a reliable car, so I just parked the thing."

It's been sitting in his barn for close to 45 years. The Greyhound is a unique and rare car, and was to be the new direction for A.C. Cars. Only 83 Greyhounds were produced from 1959 to 1963. It featured a Cobra front grill, mounted upside-down.

Instead of a 289 or 427 Ford engine—which is what Americans saw in the Cobras shipped to the United States—it featured a 105-horsepower, 2-liter Bristol engine, which had been developed as an aircraft engine by BMW before World War II.

Barger's car had seen better days. The tires had sunk into the dirt floor, and I'm sure the chassis was resting directly on the dirt. Even though Brenda said she would like to push the Greyhound into a ditch, Barger is satisfied with the car just resting in his barn.

And the moral of the story? Barn-finds are not necessarily all hiding 1,000 miles from where you live—sometimes they're right next door!

CHAPTER 81
Something Lush Behind The Brush

I think a book or a television program could have been produced about the unearthing of this terrific Packard. At the very least, it certainly ranks as barn-find of the year.

The car's lucky new owner—Paul Tacy, a fourth-generation Packard enthusiast—had heard rumors of a hidden Packard in the Adirondack region for years but just chalked the stories up as mountain lore. The Adirondack State Park takes up 6.1 million acres, and because it had been the playground of wealthy New Yorkers for 100 years, there is no shortage of forgotten vehicle stories in that region.

But when a fellow collector began hearing similar stories, Tacy started to search for details. His collector friend was told a forgotten Packard was hiding in a small garage on Charlie Hill Road in Schroon Lake, New York, just 30 minutes from Tacy's house.

In May 2013, Tacy began driving down the road slowly, looking left and right for a Packard-sized building. A small garage, with an overgrown driveway, looked promising.

Tacy forged his way to the door, which had a Posted sign tacked to it. At least 6 inches of dirt and debris prevented him from opening the door, so he

Ace car-finder Paul Tacy followed up leads, cleared away small trees and brush from the garage door, and scored this 1929 Packard Runabout.
PAUL TACY

pried open a crack just big enough to wedge his hand and a small camera inside. The photo he shot was proof that this was not a wild goose chase.

Inside, hidden for probably 50 years, was a 1929 Packard Model 633 Runabout.

He contacted the owners of the property and learned the history of the car. "The Packard was bought in Glens Falls in July 1929 by a man who worked on Wall Street in Manhattan and whose family lived in New York City," says Tacy. "He always kept it at the house in Schroon Lake, which was the family's summer home, and when he died sometime in the 1960s, the family just walked away from the house and the property. They still paid the taxes on it, but they didn't go up there at all."

Tacy showed the car's owners his family's impressive Packard collection, which convinced them that the car would be going to the right buyer. By July, he returned with a truck and trailer, tools, and a tractor complete with a backhoe. Trees had grown in front of the garage door, so Tacy needed to clear those out, dig out the stumps, and rebuild a driveway.

After much toil, Tracy dragged his barn-find home, cleaned up the decades of animal waste, rebuilt the engine, and promptly won a best of show at Albany's (NY) Fall Classic Car Show.

Plans to restore it? No way!

"I'd like to start hitting the preservation classes with it," he says. "Showing it has been fun so far with all the excitement that the story generates."

Who could imagine that this tiny, overgrown garage in the Adirondack Mountains would contain a desirable vintage Packard? It was used in the area then forgotten by the family. PAUL TACY

Note: I discovered this terrific story on Hemmings Motor News Daily Newsletter. *If you would like to read the longer format story by Daniel Strohl, go to:* http://blog.hemmings.com/index.php/2013/10/24/barn-find-1929-packard-emerges-after-50-years-wins-best-in-show-its-first-time-out/

CHAPTER 82
Private Stock

"We don't leave the doors open very often," says Marc Corea, owner of MotorCarTrader.com. "We like our inventory to be private."

But leaving the doors open to his sports car showroom last April turned out to be a brilliant move. "This guy sees the Jags in the showroom and stops in," he says. "I have a 1962 Jaguar convertible at my house," said the wanderer, Erik Ferguson. "Are you interested in looking at it?"

It took Corea all of three seconds to say yes.

Ferguson's mom bought the Jaguar for $1,000 in 1975 after her family sedan was T-boned at an intersection. They took the insurance settlement and then discovered the Jag for sale at a body shop in Charlotte, North Carolina.

Ferguson and his mom drove the car sparingly for a couple of years then parked it in their barn in 1977. Ferguson had always thought about restoring the car but never got around to it.

"I drove up to the barn, and the Jag was trapped inside," Corea says. "He (Ferguson) had to move an old CJ Jeep and pull the Jag out with a tractor. But once it was outside, I realized this was pretty special."

The 3.8-liter, non-flat-floor E-Type had only 49,830 miles on the odometer. "We agreed on a price, and I had the car flat-bedded back to my shop," he says. "There was so much dirt flying off it, I wouldn't have wanted to be riding behind it."

"You can find undesirable cars all day long, but this car is special, like the Holy Grail."

Thankfully he didn't have to fight a war for it. Crusading through friendly barns is fine with Corea.

A gentleman walked into Marc Corea's sports car shop and asked if he might be interested in buying his 1962 E-Type. It had been residing in a barn for nearly 40 years. MARC COREA

CHAPTER 83
Raised On The Radio

by Mark Henderson

During the 1960s, it was common for radio and television stations to compete by running extravagant promotions. One exceedingly popular Indianapolis-based station was WIFE, known as "Lucky 13" on the AM dial. A ratings leader, WIFE had great DJs, popular music, and some fabulous contests.

In the spring of 1965, WIFE gave away a brand new Starlight Black Pontiac GTO convertible with a red interior and a white top. Few details regarding the contest are known, but Katrina Coy, of Indianapolis, was the fortunate winner. Katrina picked up her prize that April at Dave Waite Pontiac. The GTO served as a daily driver for Mrs. Coy until 1978 when she passed it along to her daughter. Strangely though, the car was then parked in a garage and never driven again. The GTO only saw the light of day when someone opened the garage door to store more paraphernalia on top of it.

In 2006, David Wittenstein was having dinner with a longtime friend in a restaurant in Broadripple, Indiana. Sometime during the conversation, David's acquaintance mentioned that his wife had a 1965 GTO that had been parked for more than 25 years. David's interest piqued, and he wanted to learn more, but his buddy's spouse wasn't interested in selling because it had been her mother's car and she wanted to have it restored. David decided to let the matter rest but then received an urgent call almost a year later. His friend's wife had decided to let the GTO go if he was interested. David immediately drove to her home and they struck a deal.

David made preparations before taking possession of the car. After some initial research, he contacted Paul Freese, of Fast Automotive, in Batesville, Indiana, for help. Paul was soon on-site with a trailer, four aired-up tires, and three strong kids. It took almost two hours to clear all the junk and debris away from the car, but eventually a neglected yet complete numbers-matching GTO convertible was unearthed. The worn, dirty, rusty Pontiac was gently pushed onto the

The 1965 "Radio Giveaway" GTO convertible was a pushed out of an Indianapolis garage after 29 years of hibernation. DAVID WITTENSTEIN

The prize GTO has now been fully restored and is enjoyed frequently by its new caretakers.

trailer and transported straight to Paul's shop to begin the difficult work of renewal.

Four years later, the full restoration was complete. The GTO was kept stock except for carburetion, which was changed from the original Quadrajet setup to a period-correct Tri-Power configuration. The 389 cubic-inch engine, four-speed transmission, and SAF-T-TRACK differential were completely refurbished using factory specs. He removed every bolt and nut on the car, then polished or replaced them. He flawlessly applied fresh base-clear paint. He installed new interior and convertible top components. The result was a beautiful re-creation of the car's former glory.

Though Mrs. Coy had given the car to her daughter, the title was never transferred. Officially, David and his wife, Pam, are actually the GTO's *second* owners. They sometimes feel as though they won that contest back in 1965. The GTO sees the light of day frequently now, and the car itself may actually be the lucky winner overall.

CHAPTER 84

Shadows In The Basement

Bill Weissman had heard rumors of a Vincent motorcycle in a Philadelphia-area basement for decades. Beginning in the 1970s, after graduating from college and employed at his first job, Weissman heard that a Vincent Black Shadow was languishing in a unique manor house in the greater Philadelphia area, but he could never get specifics.

"In the spring of 1977, I read Hunter S. Thompson's *Fear and Loathing in Las Vegas*," Weissman says. "I had heard of Vincents before, but became hooked on the idea of owning one after reading the book."

Unable to find the mysterious Philadelphia-basement Vincent, he traveled to Hershey, Pennsylvania, for the annual fall flea market. There, he purchased a 90 percent complete Vincent Rapide. But because he was also in the process of restoring a 1969 Hemi-powered Dodge Charger 500, he didn't have the time to spend on the Vincent, and eventually sold it.

A few years later, the Vincent bug bit again, and Weissman started to ask around. Again, he heard about the Vincent in the basement, and again he could not get any details.

Find the hidden Vincent! Weissman had heard the rumors of a hidden Vincent in the Philadelphia area for years. Putting together clue upon clue, he was finally able to locate it in this basement.
BILL WEISSMAN

By the mid-1980s, Weissman purchased his first Vincent Black Shadow from Vincent expert Somer Hooker, of Nashville. Later, he also purchased another Rapide and a Comet, but still, the basement bike eluded him.

A fellow Vincent enthusiast from Oregon called Weissman in the 1990s and told him he had heard rumor of a Vincent in a Philadelphia basement, and this time Weissman received vital information that narrowed his search. Weissman's resolve was renewed; his parents lived in the greater Philadelphia area, and he decided the next time he visited them, he would explore the neighborhood for the unusual manor.

Once there, as he walked the streets, there it was; he didn't have a doubt. He knocked on the door, but no answer. Then he stopped at town hall and researched the name of the owner.

He began to send notes and letters to the owner of the house but received no reply. But after he sent a Vincent Owner's Club T-shirt, he got a surprise phone call. "It was the owner of the Shadow in the basement," Weissman says. "Yes, he still had the bike, and no, he did not want to sell it. We chatted for a while, and he inquired about Vincent people he knew."

Not the news Weissman wanted, but he had finally made a connection to the mysterious bike. Over the years, Weissman stayed in touch with the Vincent's owner, and they become friends. The elderly gentleman still had hopes of restoring his old bike.

Then one day in 2013, nearly 40 years after first hearing of the bike, Weissman got a call from the gentleman. "It's time to sell the Shadow," the owner said, who went on to explain the bike was buried in his basement.

Weissman was overjoyed. Over the next couple of weeks, he disassembled the bike into its three main sections and carried them up the stairs. "I am happy to finally own it," he says. "Somehow, in the last 25 or 30 years, I started to consider it mine anyway."

CHAPTER 85
A Pair Of Forgotten Vettes, Part 1

An elderly neighbor one day mentioned to Cary Thomas that his son, Ron, used to race Corvettes. Thomas didn't think much of it until December 2011, when the neighbor mentioned that Ron wanted to sell his Corvettes.

Ron was ill and in the middle of a divorce. His wife got the house, and Ron got the two Corvettes. The trouble was that they were trapped in a garage; the doors didn't function, and there was a chance they would fall on the two sports cars. How to get them out?

"Garage door mechanics wouldn't touch the job," says Thomas, 65, from Carlsbad, California. But luckily, he went there with five buddies, one of whom repaired garage doors. As they exhumed the cars, neighbors started coming over and commenting, "We had heard there were Corvettes in there."

The brakes were frozen and the tires were flat, but eventually, they were loaded onto trailers. Thomas decided to keep the 1967 427 coupe. It had an L71, four-speed, and a suspension that had been worked on by Dick Guildstrand. The "gas tank sticker" was still in good shape, and it only had 62,000 miles on the odometer.

"The car had a roll bar; Ron used to autocross and drag-race the car," he says.

So far, Thomas has oiled down the cylinders and still needs to install new tires and brakes. But he's going to take his friends' advice and leave the car as a survivor.

What about the other Corvette? Well, turn the page.

Cary Thomas heard from his neighbor that his son was getting a divorce and needed to sell his two Corvettes. The garage had to be partially dismantled to reveal the booty inside.
CARY THOMAS

CHAPTER 86
A Pair Of Forgotten Vettes, Part 2

There were *two* cars in Ron's broken down garage—remember?

Cary Thomas negotiated to remove two Corvettes that had been ignored for many years. Of the two cars, he decided to keep the big-block 1967 coupe.

The other one? A 1965 Corvette convertible racecar.

The long-time owner of the two cars, named Ron, bought and raced the car until putting it in long-time storage. Before buying the Vette racer, a previous owner had been killed in the car when the car was T-boned in a race by a Sunbeam Tiger. Thomas had no desire to keep the racer and advertised it on eBay in the summer of 2012.

"I started corresponding with him," says Joe Hofman, 52, of San Diego. "The Buy-It-Now price was $25,000. Nobody was really bidding on it, so after it didn't sell at auction, I went up to look at it."

What Hofman found didn't scare him. He had owned several Corvettes in the past and was looking for a vintage racecar. What he bought was an authentic historic racer. "It's not really that modified," he says. "The car is very original and has some pretty rare cylinder heads."

Hofman restored the Corvette's drivetrain and chassis, but he left the body as it was when removed from the garage-tomb. The paint is still red, but some of the white and blue from decades earlier was sanded off.

"I'm entered at the Monterey Historics," he says. "It's exciting to return the car to the track." Hopefully it performs just as well, too.

This racing Sting Ray had been entombed inside this tiny garage for decades. Tearing down the wall revealed the cars.

Joe Hoffman restored the former racecar mechanically but left much of its cosmetic patina.

XIV

OF HEART-WARMERS AND STREETWALKERS

CHAPTER 87
Earnhardt's Dumper

Lars Ekberg invited me to his home in North Carolina to show me his great cars, some of which were barn-finds. As we walked from garage to garage, we kept passing a big old Ford dump truck, nasty and neglected. I didn't pay any attention to it.

As I was about to say thank you and goodbye, Ekberg said to me, "You know, that old truck has an interesting story. It used to belong to Dale Earnhardt, Senior."

I stopped in my tracks. "Can you tell me more?" I asked.

"My buddy Jimmy Sides went to school with Dale," he said. "They were lifelong friends."

Ekberg explained that Earnhardt had owned the 1967 F-600 truck for a long time and had used it at his nearby farm in Mooresville, North Carolina, to haul around hay for horses. Sides bought it from Dale about 20 years ago to use when feeding his own horses, but parked it in a barn about 15 years ago and never took it out again.

"When Jimmy passed away in 2010, his wife called me up and asked if I wanted the old truck," Ekberg said. "She gave it to me. The title is still in Dale's name."

So there the truck continues to sit, last inspected in 2000. Ekberg is undecided what he will do with the old relic. But one thing is for certain—he owns the world's largest Dale Earnhardt souvenir.

When seven-time NASCAR Champ Dale Earnhardt wasn't driving around the track in his famous #3 Chevy, he was hauling hay around the farm in this 1967 Ford F-600 dump truck.
TOM COTTER

CHAPTER 88

A Passion Renewed

Sergio Arredondo bought an Iso Grifo, a terrific Italian-American hybrid sports car, back in 1982. This 1969 beauty was sitting at a used car lot north of Los Angeles.

"My company was doing a construction project at the dealership," says the 67-year-old Arredondo, from Pasadena, California. "I saw the Iso for sale and I fell in love. I took it for a ride, and five days later, it was sitting in my driveway."

Even many hard-core enthusiasts have never seen or heard of an Iso Grifo, and that's understandable. Only 413 were built in Italy between 1963 and 1974 by the Iso Rivolta Company. The beautiful Bertone-designed 2+2 coupe was powered by a variety of American V-8s: 327, 427, or 454 Chevy or 351 Ford. Automatic, four-speed, and five-speed transmissions were available.

The Iso Grifo's competition highlight was a 14th place finish at the 1964 24 Hours of LeMans. But the car's strength was never racing; instead, it was a gentleman's touring car.

Arredondo bought the beautiful, 327-horsepower burgundy sports car when his oldest son, Chris, was just one year old. His younger son, Antonio, wasn't even born yet. "I've always owned a sports car as well as a sedan," Arredondo says. "I paid about $21,000 for it. I drove it on weekends for about five years."

Then it was parked. He took off his leather driving gloves and placed them on the shifter.

Sergio Arredondo got busy with business and politics, parked his 1969 Iso Grifo in the garage, and basically forgot about it for the next quarter-century. SERGIO ARREDONDO

Through the urging of his sons, Sergio pulled it into the daylight again! SERGIO ARREDONDO

Arredondo, the owner of two businesses, was appointed to leadership positions in local, then national politics. "I worked with presidents, governors, and senators, and I would be away from home for months at a time," he says. "I no longer had time for all my toys. I didn't need them; I was too busy."

He backed his beautiful Iso Grifo into the garage, closed the door, and basically forgot he even owned it. Then one day a couple of decades later, Arredondo was watching the Barrett-Jackson Auctions, and an Iso Grifo went across the block.

"Dad, that's just like your Iso in the garage," said his son Chris. Chris also encouraged him to join the Iso Owners Club. He attended an Iso-themed display at The Quail car show Concorso Italiano in conjunction with the Pebble Beach Concours in August 2013.

A word from his son was all it took—the flame was re-lit. "I was like, 'Hey, look what I discovered in my garage,'" he says. "I'm going to take that car out and drive it again! It was dirty and filthy, so my sons and I washed and waxed it."

He brought the car to a shop recommended by one of the Iso Club members. The mechanic got the engine running and began the process of cosmetic restoration and minor repairs of the engine. "The interior doesn't look bad and the paint is pretty good, so I think I'll just drive the car for a while," he says.

He intends to add Weber carburetors and has already ordered a set of chrome Borrani wire wheels. One thing he won't have to order is driving gloves. They were still sitting on the shifter, exactly where he left them 24 years earlier.

CHAPTER 89

SS Surprise Party

by Wes Eisenschenk

When Wally Eisenschenk was a teenager, he owned a 1969 Impala 327. His younger brother, Joe, also liked Impalas. In the late '70s, Wally asked Joe if he would have an interest in an SS he had found near Brainerd, Minnesota. This was no ordinary SS— it was a 427 convertible sporting Garnet Red paint with a Parchment interior. The Chevy wasn't road worthy, but with a little TLC, it could be.

Joe made the purchase but soon ran into financial difficulties due to an impending divorce; the bank repossessed the SS before he ever got a chance to drive it. With sentiment on his mind, Joe cunningly removed all the SS badges off the car as souvenirs. Like any jealous brother, my dad, Wally, jotted down the VIN off the Impala and stowed the piece of paper in his wallet just in case he would someday have his date with destiny.

As Dad approached his 50th birthday, my brother, sister, and I wanted to do something special for him. The idea stumbled upon me to pick his brain about the old SS. He confirmed that he still knew the

Wes Eisenschenk and his siblings decided to try to locate and buy back the SS 427 Impala their father, Wally, owned as a young man. This is the car they presented him at his surprise 50th birthday party. WES EISENSCHENK

Today, eight years later, Wally's 427 convertible has been restored to as-new condition, down to the original drivetrain. WES EISENSCHENK

whereabouts of the car and even opened up his wallet to show me the name of the owner and the location where it was being stored. While he was asleep one night, I plundered his wallet and found the holy grail of Impala contact information. I reached out to the facility, but the record keeper would not disclose if the car was there or who owned it. I suggested that "if" the car was there, could she possibly contact the individual who owned the car to see if they would be interested in selling?

Three weeks later I finally got the call I was waiting for. The current owner was willing to sell solely based on the family history of the car. We struck up a deal with each sibling kicking in one-third of the agreed upon sum of $3,600. For the next 18 months we kept the Impala at the storage facility and our mouths shut.

As a diversion, we staged a surprise 50th birthday party for Dad. Halfway through the party, a friend

snuck off to where we had stuffed the Impala. Moments later, the SS could be seen peering over the tops of people's heads sporting a 3-foot wide bow tie, waiting for Dad to catch a glimpse of it. I could see a haunting look overcome my dad as he caught a glimpse of the car in midconversation with a friend. The place was buzzing and there was applause as people parted while dad slowly made his way toward the SS.

It's hard to believe that eight years have passed since the unveiling of the Impala at dad's 50th birthday party. The Chevy has been restored back to original and retains the factory-correct driveline. With the original emblems back on the car, Wally took his brother Joe out on his long-awaited first ride.

CHAPTER 90
The Old Lady And The Continental

"I've been screwing with old Porsches since I was 16," Chris Stavros says. "I'm 56 now."

When Stavros told me that at the beginning of our interview, I figured he knew his way around a metric tool set. Just one month earlier, in May 2013, he got a call from a friend who worked with Starvos at a Porsche dealership in the 1980s.

"He told me he got a call from an old lady, probably 80 years old, whose husband used to race Porsches," he says. "She told him, 'I'm moving to Huntington Beach to a retirement community. I need to sell my Porsche.'"

Her Porsche was a 1955 Continental Coupe that became hers when she and her husband got divorced in 1970, when it was last registered. Prior to then, she drove the car daily when she sold Tupperware. "There was crap packed all over the car, so if the garage door was open, you'd never know a Porsche was in there."

"Would you be interested?" the woman asked Stavros.

The car had matching engine numbers and the only repair he noticed was in the rear clip from when the woman was rear-ended. "I had a devil on one shoulder and an angel on the other," Stavros says. "She had no idea what the car was worth."

Chris Stavros got a call about a woman who needed to sell her 1955 Porsche Continental because she was moving into an assisted care facility. She had once delivered Tupperware in this car! CHRIS STAVROS

He made her a market-value offer, and she accepted. The Jade metallic green Porsche now sits in his garage next to a Speedster in the same color.

"What are the chances to find two barn-find Porsches in exactly the same, non-factory color?" he wonders.

Somehow, the more of these stories I hear, the more likely they seem.

CHAPTER 91
Meet You Out Back

Just as you can't judge a book by its cover, you can't judge a used car dealer by its front row.

Even though the Virginia dealership had shiny, late model cars up front, a shed in the back of the lot hid at least one desirable treasure.

Ace Ford barn-finder Lars Ekberg had heard about a 1963 1/2 R-Code fastback at the Virginia car dealer. It was out of sight, stored in a shed with several other older cars. The dealer had purchased the car in 1977 from the original owner in Charlotte, North Carolina. Ekberg was told it had been frequently street-raced "back in the day."

The Galaxy sat in the dealer shed for at least 20 years. This car was particularly desirable because it was an R-Code, meaning that it had built with Ford's 427 cubic-inch engine; very powerful and very rare. The car also came equipped with a four-speed gearbox, XL trim, and had only 77,000 original miles.

The original owner replaced the 427 emblems with 390 cubic-inch emblems, probably to fool potential street-racing competitors. Eventually, he blew the 427 engine and replaced it with a less-powerful 352 engine, but the car wound up sitting in a field behind the owner's home.

Lars Ekberg followed up leads about this 1963 1/2 R-Code Galaxy sitting in a shed at a Virginia used car dealership. LARS EKBERG

Ekberg successfully purchased the car with the intention of restoring it to original, but eventually he had to sell it to a Virginia enthusiast who lived just 20 miles from the car dealership where it sat for so many years.

"The buyer wanted to restore it and bring it to the Barrett-Jackson auction," Ekberg says. "I'm not sure if that ever happened."

CHAPTER 92

Smooth Operator

It is difficult to comprehend that a man—one stricken with Alzheimer's disease and living in a nursing facility, no less—was the original owner of one of the most powerful muscle cars ever built: a Boss 429 Mustang. Car guys should be exempt from turning old.

The owner, now unable to care for himself, once proudly waxed the car's gorgeous Black Jade paint job and power-shifted the car through the gears at traffic lights. He still loved the car, but he had other priorities.

This was the situation Mark Rubin had to navigate when he approached the man's family to buy the car. The Boss had been their elderly father's pride and joy since new, but rising medical care costs forced the family to consider selling.

The powerful Mustang "was not the prettiest girl at the dance," he says. "It sat for at least 25 years under a tarp." The car's original dark green paint was pocked with factory red oxide primer as a result of sitting so long under the bleaching sun.

"It took me five months to convince them to sell the car," Rubin says. "Needless to say, this was not merely a sale of a car, but the handing over of decades of memories. I was happy with the final results; I was able to buy the car, but I was even happier that their father would be properly cared for through his final days."

Rubin discovered the car was purchased new at Don Kott Ford in Carson, California; the engine,

This Boss 429 Mustang sat for over 25 years under a tarp. Ouch.

Hard to let a logo as iconic as this one go—despite being urged to leave the patina as-is, Rubin restored the car to its former splendor.

After a little digging, Rubin discovered the engine, transmission, rear, shocks, exhaust, and interior were all numbers-matching correct.

transmission, rear, shocks, exhaust, and interior were original and numbers-matching.

"It was definitely the most original car I ever owned," he says. "Every body panel is original and completely solid: fenders, doors, quarter panels, floors, aprons, everything as it left the factory in 1969. The interior was in great condition, and I only replaced the dash pad with an NOS one that I received with the car."

Due to a valve issue, the top half of the engine was partially disassembled when Rubin purchased the car. However, the car's trunk housed every piece of the disassembled top half of the engine along with a treasure trove of NOS gaskets and other extra NOS Boss 429 specific items: air cleaner, exhaust manifolds, distributor, export brace, and radiator are all original and accounted for. The car also has the

original aluminum engine tag, buck tag, multiple buildsheets, and original factory order invoices.

For a long time, Rubin was undecided on whether to restore the car or not.

The car was invited to appear on an episode of Discovery Channel's *What's My Car Worth?* Show hosts Keith Martin and Bill Stephens suggested that Rubin restore the rare Mustang. But classic car insurer McKeel Hagerty pleaded that the car be left original.

"McKeel felt the car had wonderful patina and that its cosmetics gave it real character," Rubin says. Despite Hagerty's suggestion, Rubin decided to go the restoration route.

"I can tell you this: when the car was displayed at the Petersen Museum prior to restoration, it drew large crowds all day." As well it should.

CHAPTER 93

Push The Bush For A Superbird

Barry Lee is brilliant. The motorcycle dealer from Jacksonville, Florida, disguised a barn-finding adventure as a romantic weekend with his wife at a casino in Biloxi, Mississippi.

Lee had heard of a rare and desirable Plymouth Superbird behind a house in Alabama, which he could visit en route.

"I told my wife we would go gambling over Christmas," said Lee. "She was all for it!"

Lee's profession is two-wheelers, but his passion is very fast four-wheelers of the Mopar variety. He had already owned a number of big-block 'Cudas, Super Bees and Challengers, but his dream was for one of Chryslers high-winged models: the Superbird or its cousin, the Dodge Daytona, cars designed to compete on NASCAR's superspeedways with drivers like Richard Petty and Bobby Allison.

He heard from an unreliable source about a Superbird that had been sitting behind a house near the Gulf Coast since 1975.

After a terrific holiday weekend of gambling, the happy couple drove through the coastal Alabama town and to the address where the automotive treasure was supposedly sitting.

The house was obviously abandoned, and the property was littered with old trucks and cars, but there was no Superbird. Lee was beginning to think his friend was pulling his leg when his wife noticed an orange object inside a nearby bush. When her husband pushed aside the branches, it revealed the car of this dreams—a bright orange, 1970 Plymouth Superbird. Parked in the same location for three decades, a hedge had actually engulfed the car.

Find the hidden Superbird! At first, Barry Lee didn't even see the car he had heard about in an Alabama yard. It had been parked behind a house for nearly 30 years, and eventually the hedge grew up around it.
BARRY LEE

Parked in a barn near Lee's house in Jacksonville, Florida, the car reveals its rough condition. Even the firewall has cancer. Yet Lee looks forward to the ultimate restoration.

All those years parked in the salty, humid air near the Alabama coast took its toll on the rare Plymouth. According to Lee, nearly every metal panel needs repair or replacement.
BARRY LEE

Lee found out who owned the house and called the phone number. "Whenever I called and said I was interested in the car, the person on the other end hung up the phone," said Lee.

It turns out the elderly owner, Frank Moran, whose wife was in a nursing home, lived nearby with his daughter.

So Lee's wife stepped in again and suggested they simply write a letter that stated their desire to remove the car from the elements and restore it like new.

At least a year passed before Lee received a surprise phone call from Frank's son-in-law, George Proux.

"Frank fell and is in the hospital," Proux said. "I have power-of-attorney and had all the cars and trucks hauled off before I found your letter.

"The Superbird is sitting at my house in Jacksonville, Florida."

What a coincidence that it should actually be just a few miles from Lee's own house.

Lee carefully inspected the car. It was equipped with a numbers-matching 440 cubic-inch engine, automatic transmission and bench seat, and still wore its original Goodyear Wide Oval tires on rally rims.

It was one of only 1,920 Superbirds that year, and incredibly, this one had less than 1,000 miles on it.

The son-in-law had planned to restore the car, but after surveying the severe rust damage, he reconsidered.

Lee arrived at just the right moment: he had driven his own 1970 lime-green Road Runner, which attracted Proux's attention.

The two traded cars and Lee now owns possibly the lowest-mileage Superbird on the planet. A major restoration in in progress.

CHAPTER 94

Winged Quonset Discovery

I know it's tough for most of us to accept, but folks in the old car business hear about more old-car deals than you and I do.

I mean, who's going to hear about more old cars, an accountant or someone in the restoration business?

So, like it or not, Tony Dagostino of Harrington, Delaware, has one leg up on the rest of us.

Dagostino owns Tony's Mopar Parts, a supplier of NOS, used and high-quality reproduction parts for Chrysler muscle cars. It's a business the 50-year-old has been in since he was 14.

"It was a hobby that became my business," he said. "I bought a 1970 Road Runner when I was a kid, and I found myself in business. I still own that car today."

A few years ago, Dagostino received a phone call from a customer about a 1969 Dodge Daytona that had been parked in a Louisville, Kentucky, Quonset hut from 1976 until 2005. The customer wanted to buy the car and flip it for a profit but wanted Dagostino to check it over first.

From a distance, both the Dodge Daytona and the Plymouth Superbird look similar; pointed nose and tall rear wing. But the Daytona is a much rarer find. Only 503 were manufactured in order to homologate the car for NASCAR. According to Dagostino, the car was designed to the very highest aerodynamic standards at the time.

The Superbird, on the other hand, was produced at a higher volume: 1,920 were built, roughly one for

Tony Dagostino, who makes his living selling NOS MOPAR parts, heard from a customer about this Dodge Daytona sitting neglected in a Louisville, Kentucky, Quonset hut. TONY DAGOSTINO

Dagostino bought the 50,000-mile car, which had been sitting in the shed since 1976. TONY DAGOSTINO

The Dodge Daytona has since been restored to Concours standards.

every other Plymouth dealer in the country. And according to Dagostino, they were not quite as good in stock form.

"The Daytonas did not come with vinyl tops or air conditioning," he said. "They were assembled by Creative Industries, where the fenders, hood, trunk, grill, and bumpers were replaced. And the rear window was mounted flush to the body."

The '69 Daytona Dagostino heard about had incurred door damage from a minor accident in 1976 and wouldn't shut. So the owner simply parked the 50,000-mile car.

When the car went on sale, it changed hands a couple of times in just few days, until it arrived in Dagostino's garage.

"Everyone was flipping it to make some money," he said.

He was particularly impressed with the car's original colors, white with a red wing and red interior.

The car was equipped with a 440 cubic-inch, four-barrel carburetor, and automatic transmission.

Dagostino restored the car to the highest standards, even sourcing correct date-code seat fabric.

"I was lucky," he said. "The car had zero rust, except for a little corrosion in the passenger floor area where the mice had built a huge hotel. Their urine ate a hole through the floor."

The car was restored using the best products Dagostino could source: NOS heater hoses; trunk mat; tires; wheels; shocks; and any correct, authentic part he could locate.

Since its completion, the car has won a gold medal at the Mopar Nationals, the highest award at the Chicago Muscle Car Nationals (999 out of 1,000 points) and has been displayed at Chrysler Carlisle.

But it's now too perfect to drive.

"It's my full-scale model," Dagostino said.

INDEX